"*Your Word* Is a Lamp to My Foot"

"Your word is a lamp to my foot,
and a light to my roadway."
—Ps. 119:105.

PUBLISHERS
WATCHTOWER BIBLE AND TRACT SOCIETY
OF NEW YORK, INC.
INTERNATIONAL BIBLE STUDENTS ASSOCIATION
Brooklyn, New York, U.S.A.

Made in the United States of America

Dedicated

to the

"Father of the Celestial Lights,"
who is the divine Giver of the
"lamp" for our foot
and
in whose lighted roadway we should walk
by full dedication and water baptism
in the footsteps of Jesus Christ

CONTENTS

CHAPTER 1

Basic Teachings of the Bible

J EHOVAH GOD has lovingly provided his written Word the Bible to reveal himself to mankind. In it he tells us of the things that he has done, his purposes for the future and what we must do to walk in harmony with his will. If you are to be one of Jehovah's Christian witnesses, these are things that you should know so that you can properly represent God before your fellowmen.

The Bible plainly states that God's will is for people to "come to an accurate knowledge of truth." (1 Tim. 2:4) Such knowledge is necessary in order to walk in a way that pleases Jehovah. That is why the apostle Paul, who was deeply interested in the spiritual welfare of other people, wrote on one occasion: "We . . . have not ceased praying for you and asking that you may be filled with the accurate knowledge of his will in all wisdom and spiritual discernment, in order to walk worthily of Jehovah to the end of fully pleasing him." (Col. 1:9, 10) Are you equipped with such accurate knowledge?

To teach others about God and to walk worthily of Jehovah yourself, you need to be equipped with knowledge. That is why we strongly recommend that anyone who plans to get baptized come to an accurate knowledge of at least the basic teachings of the Bible first. This is in harmony with Jesus' instructions to make disciples of people and then to baptize them. (Matt. 28:19) A disciple is one who learns and accepts the teachings of another.

Have you learned and accepted the fundamental teachings set out in the Bible?

We believe that you will be greatly aided to do so if you read the books *"Things in Which It Is Impossible for God to Lie"* and *Life Everlasting— in Freedom of the Sons of God* (or, if they are not available in your language, other recent publications of the Watch Tower Bible and Tract Society that cover similar material). In this way you will find out what the Bible teaches, what Jehovah's Christian witnesses advocate and the responsibilities that you are accepting when you get baptized.

Before each assembly of Jehovah's Christian witnesses, at which arrangements are made for immersion of those who qualify, your congregation overseer will check to ascertain whether there are any associated with the congregation who are planning to get baptized. If there are, he will ask them if they have read the publications mentioned in the preceding paragraph. If they have not yet done so, he will urge them to complete that reading before they are baptized. He will also arrange to have a series of meetings with these candidates for immersion to review the information that follows under this heading "Basic Teachings of the Bible." This will help them to be sure that they really understand these important matters and it will assure the congregation that those who get baptized really know what is involved in being one of Jehovah's Christian witnesses and that they Scripturally qualify for immersion.

Baptism is an important step in your life, and not one to be taken lightly. If you plan to be immersed, you should arrange your personal affairs so that you do not miss any of these preliminary meetings for baptismal candidates. In preparation, it would be wise to review the questions on the following pages and read the material that is provided in answer. Also, look up any scriptures that are cited but not quoted. Do not try to memorize answers. The important thing is to be sure that you understand each point, that you believe it and that you are able to express it clearly. Analyze how each thought affects your own life. Keep in mind that the reason for learning these truths well is so that you can "walk worthily of Jehovah to the end of fully pleasing him."

The material outlined on pages 7 to 40 will be divided between three or more sessions, at the discretion of the congregation overseer. He will conduct at least one of the sessions himself, and, if he chooses to do so, he may arrange for the other sessions to be presided over by other members of the congregation committee or other mature brothers designated by him. These meetings are not meant to embarrass anyone, but to give each one opportunity to express the things that he sincerely believes. The apostle Paul said there should be "an interchange of encouragement among you, by each one through the other's faith, both yours and mine." (Rom. 1:12) These meetings provide a fine opportunity for some of the appointed servants to become well acquainted with you and, in turn, for you to come to know them so that you feel free to approach them. If there are any points that you do not fully understand, do not hesitate to say so. These brothers will be glad to help.

Together, now, let us review these basic teachings of the Bible, one at a time, and let us try to understand and also to express in our own words what these scriptures mean to us.

Who is the true God?

The Bible answers: "That people may know that you, whose name is Jehovah, you alone are the Most High over all the earth." (Ps. 83:18) "Listen, O Israel: Jehovah our God is one Jehovah." (Deut. 6:4; Mark 12:

29) "God is a Spirit, and those worshiping him must worship with spirit and truth." (John 4:24) [Consider how this differs from local popular beliefs, whether of Christendom or of other religions.]

What kind of God is Jehovah?

"God is love." (1 John 4:8) "The Rock, perfect is his activity, for all his ways are justice. A God of faithfulness, with whom there is no injustice; righteous and upright is he." (Deut. 32:4) "O the depth of God's riches and wisdom and knowledge! How unsearchable his judgments are and past tracing out his ways are!" (Rom. 11:33) "O Lord Jehovah! Here you yourself have made the heavens and the earth by your great power and by your outstretched arm. The whole matter is not too wonderful for you yourself." (Jer. 32:17) "No man has seen God at any time; the only-begotten god who is in the bosom position with the Father is the one that has explained him." (John 1:18) "Jehovah went passing by before his face and declaring: 'Jehovah, Jehovah, a God merciful and gracious, slow to anger and abundant in loving-kindness and truth, preserving loving-kindness for thousands, pardoning error and transgression and sin, but by no means will he give exemption from punishment.'" (Ex. 34:6, 7) "Jehovah is not slow respecting his promise, as some people consider slowness, but he is patient with you because he does not desire any to be destroyed but desires all to attain to repentance." (2 Pet. 3:9) "Before the mountains themselves were born, or you proceeded to bring forth as with labor pains the earth and the productive land, even from time indefinite to time indefinite you are God." (Ps. 90:2)

What does the Bible mean when it says that Jehovah requires our exclusive devotion?

"In reply Jesus said to him: 'It is written, "It is Jehovah your God you must worship, and it is to him alone you must render sacred service."'" (Luke 4:8) "You must not make for yourself a carved image or a form like anything that is in the heavens above or that is on the earth underneath or that is in the waters under the earth. You must not bow down to them nor be induced to serve them, because I Jehovah your God am a God exacting exclusive devotion." (Ex. 20:4, 5)

How will Jehovah God sanctify his name? How can we have a share in it?

"I will bring myself into judgment with him, with pestilence and with blood; . . . And I shall certainly magnify myself and sanctify myself and make myself known before the eyes of many nations; and they will have to know that I am Jehovah." (Ezek. 38:22, 23) "You must pray, then, this way: 'Our Father in the heavens, let your name be sanctified.'" (Matt. 6:9) "Jehovah of armies—he is the One whom you should treat as holy." (Isa. 8:13) "I have glorified you on the earth . . . I have made your name manifest to the men you gave me out of the world." (John 17:4, 6) "Maintain your conduct fine among the nations, that, in the thing in which they are speaking against you as evildoers, they may as a result of your fine works of which they are eyewitnesses glorify God in the day for his inspection." (1 Pet. 2:12) [Consider how one's conduct reflects on Jehovah's name.]

Who is Jesus Christ?

"In answer Simon Peter said: 'You are the Christ, the Son of the living God.'" (Matt. 16:16)

What is Jesus' position in relation to Jehovah God?

"You heard that I said to you, I am going away and I am coming back to you. If you loved me, you would rejoice that I am going my way to the Father, because the Father is greater than I am." (John 14:28) "He is the image of the invisible God, the first-born of all creation; because by means of him all other things were created in the heavens and upon the earth, the things visible and the things invisible, no matter whether they are thrones or lordships or governments or authorities. All other things have been created through him and for him. Also, he is before all other things and by means of him all other things were made to exist." (Col. 1:15-17) "There is one God, and one mediator between God and men, a man Christ Jesus." (1 Tim. 2:5) "Keep this mental attitude in you that was also in Christ Jesus, who, although he was existing in God's form, gave no consideration to a seizure, namely, that he should be equal to God. No, but he emptied himself and took a slave's form and came to be in the likeness of men. More than that, when he found himself in fashion as a man, he humbled himself and became obedient as far as death, yes, death on a torture stake. For this very reason also God exalted him to a superior position and kindly gave him the name that is above every other name, so that in the name of Jesus every knee should bend of those in heaven and those on earth and those under the ground, and every tongue should openly acknowledge that Jesus Christ is Lord to the glory of God the Father." (Phil. 2:5-11)

Why did Jesus die a sacrificial death?

"The Son of man came, not to be ministered to, but to minister and to give his soul a ransom in exchange for many." (Matt. 20:28) "We behold Jesus, who has been made a little lower than angels, crowned with glory and honor for having suffered death, that he by God's undeserved kindness might taste death for every man. . . . that through his death he might bring to nothing the one having the means to cause death, that is, the Devil; and that he might emancipate all those who for fear of death were subject to slavery all through their lives." (Heb. 2:9, 14, 15) "The next day he beheld Jesus coming toward him, and he said: 'See, the Lamb of God that takes away the sin of the world!'" (John 1:29)

How is the ransom an expression of God's love for mankind?

"God recommends his own love to us in that, while we were yet sinners, Christ died for us." (Rom. 5:8) "By this the love of God was made manifest in our case, because God sent forth his only-begotten Son into the world that we might gain life through him. The love is in this respect, not that we have loved God, but that he loved us and sent forth his Son as a propitiatory sacrifice for our sins." (1 John 4:9, 10) "God loved the world so much that he gave his only-begotten Son, in order that everyone exercising faith in him might not be destroyed but have everlasting life." (John 3:16)

How does the ransom affect us as individuals?

"By means of him we have the release by ransom through the blood of that one, yes, the forgiveness of our trespasses, according to the riches of his undeserved kindness." (Eph. 1:7) "My little children, I am writing you these things that you may not commit a sin. And yet, if anyone does commit a sin, we have a helper with the Father, Jesus Christ, a righteous one. And he is a propitiatory sacrifice for our sins, yet not for ours only but also for the whole world's." (1 John 2:1, 2) "He that exercises faith in the Son has ever-lasting life; he that disobeys the Son will not see life, but the wrath of God remains upon him." (John 3:36)

What is the holy spirit?

"God's *active force* was moving to and fro over the surface of the waters." (Gen. 1:2) "You will receive power when the holy spirit arrives upon you, and you will be witnesses of me both in Jerusalem and in all Judea and Samaria and to the most distant part of the earth." (Acts 1:8) "Now while the day of the festival of Pentecost was in progress they were all together at the same place, and suddenly there occurred from heaven a noise just like that of a rushing stiff breeze, and it filled the whole house in which they were sitting. And tongues as if of fire became visible to them and were distributed about, and one sat upon each one of them, and they all became filled with holy spirit and started to speak with different tongues, just as the spirit was granting them to make utterance." (Acts 2:1-4)

How can we benefit from the operation of that spirit today?

"If you, although being wicked, know how to give good gifts to your children, how much more so will the Father in heaven give holy spirit to those asking him!" (Luke 11:13) "All Scripture is *inspired* of God and beneficial for teaching, for reproving, for setting things straight, for disciplining in righteousness." (2 Tim. 3:16; see also 2 Peter 1:21.) "Pay attention to your-selves and to all the flock, among which the holy spirit has appointed you overseers, to shepherd the congrega-tion of God, which he purchased with the blood of his own Son." (Acts 20:28)

Whose ideas are recorded in the Bible? Does that mean that God personally spoke or wrote it all? Is all of it true?

"All Scripture is inspired of God." (2 Tim. 3:16) "Indeed, that is why we also thank God incessantly, because when you received God's word, which you heard from us, you accepted it, not as the word of men, but, just as it truthfully is, as the word of God, which is also at work in you believers." (1 Thess. 2:13) "You know this first, that no prophecy of Scripture springs from any private interpretation. For prophecy was at no time brought by man's will, but men spoke from God as they were borne along by holy spirit." (2 Pet. 1:20, 21) "Sanctify them by means of the truth; your word is truth." (John 17:17)

Why should we pray?

"The end of all things has drawn close. Be sound in mind, therefore, and be vigilant with a view to prayers." (1 Pet. 4:7) "Then he went on to tell them an illustration with regard to the need for them always to pray and not to give up." (Luke 18:1) "Pray for one another . . . A righteous man's supplication, when it is at work, has much force." (Jas. 5:16)

To whom should we pray?

"If you ask the Father for anything he will give it to you in my name. . . . Ask and you will receive, that your joy may be made full." (John 16:23, 24) "To my sayings do give ear, O Jehovah; do understand my sighing. Do pay attention to the sound of my cry for help, O my King and my God, because to you I pray." (Ps. 5:1, 2)

About what is it proper to pray?

"No matter what it is that we ask according to his will, he hears us." (1 John 5:14) "Do not be anxious over anything, but in everything by prayer and supplication along with thanksgiving let your petitions be made known to God." (Phil. 4:6) "In the name of our Lord Jesus Christ giving thanks always for all things to our God and Father." (Eph. 5:20) "You must pray, then, this way: 'Our Father in the heavens, let your name be sanctified. Let your kingdom come. Let your will take place, as in heaven, also upon earth. Give us today our bread for this day; and forgive us our debts, as we also have forgiven our debtors. And do not bring us into temptation, but deliver us from the wicked one.'" (Matt. 6:9-13)

What is the kingdom of God?

"I kept on beholding in the visions of the night, and, see there! with the clouds of the heavens someone like a son of man happened to be coming; and to the Ancient of Days he gained access, and they brought him up close even before that One. And to him there were given rulership and dignity and kingdom, that the peoples, national groups and languages should all serve even him. His rulership is an indefinitely lasting rulership that will not pass away, and his kingdom one that will not be brought to ruin." (Dan. 7:13, 14) "In the days of those kings the God of heaven will set up a kingdom that will never be brought to ruin. And the kingdom itself will not be passed on to any other people. It will crush and put an end to all these kingdoms, and it itself will stand to times indefinite." (Dan. 2:44) "Jesus answered: 'My kingdom is no part of this world. If my kingdom were part of this world, my attendants would have fought that I should not be delivered up to the Jews. But, as it is, my kingdom is not from this source.'" (John 18:36) "They sing a new song, saying: 'You are worthy to take the scroll and open its seals, because you were slaughtered and with your blood you bought persons for God out of every tribe and tongue and people and nation, and you made them to be a kingdom and priests to our God, and they will rule as kings over the earth." (Rev. 5:9, 10)

When Christ returns, is it visibly as a man, or how?

"When the Son of man arrives in his glory, and all the angels with him, then he will sit down on his glorious throne." (Matt. 25:31) "Christ died once for all time concerning sins, a righteous person for unrighteous ones, that he might lead you to God, he being put to death in the flesh, but being made alive in the spirit." (1 Pet. 3:18) "In the house of my Father there are many abodes. Otherwise, I would have told you, because I am going my way to prepare a place for you. Also, if I go my way and prepare a place for you, I am coming again and will receive you home to myself, that where I am you also may be. A little longer and the world will behold me no more, but you will behold me, because I live and you will live." (John 14:2, 3, 19)

How can people know when his second presence takes place?

Read in your copy of the Bible the entire chapters of Matthew 24, 25; Mark 13; Luke 21; Daniel 4; Revelation 6.

What does it mean to 'seek first the kingdom'?

"Stop storing up for yourselves treasures upon the earth, where moth and rust consume, and where thieves break in and steal. Rather, store up for yourselves treasures in heaven, where neither moth nor rust consumes, and where thieves do not break in and steal. . . . No one can slave for two masters; for either he will hate the one and love the other, or he will stick to the one and despise the other. You cannot slave for God and for Riches. . . . So never be anxious and say, 'What are we to eat?' or, 'What are we to drink?' or, 'What are we to put on?' For all these are the things the nations are eagerly pursuing. For your heavenly Father knows you need all these things. Keep on, then, seeking first the kingdom and his righteousness, and all these other things will be added to you." (Matt. 6:19-33) "So, then, because we have so great a cloud of witnesses surrounding us, let us also put off every weight and the sin that easily entangles us, and let us run with endurance the race that is set before us, as we look intently at the Chief Agent and Perfecter of our faith, Jesus. For the joy that was set before him he endured a torture stake, despising shame, and has sat down at the right hand of the throne of God. Indeed, consider closely the one who has endured such contrary talk by sinners against their own interests, that you may not get tired and give out in your souls." (Heb. 12:1-3) "When they got to him he said to them: 'You well know how from the first day that I stepped into the district of Asia I was with you the whole time, slaving for the Lord with the greatest lowliness of mind and tears and trials that befell me by the plots of the Jews; while I did not hold back from telling you any of the things that were profitable nor from teaching you publicly and from house to house. But I thoroughly bore witness both to Jews and to Greeks about repentance toward God and faith in our Lord Jesus.'" (Acts 20: 18-21) "This good news of the kingdom will be preached in all the inhabited earth for a witness to all the nations; and then the end will come." (Matt. 24:14)

What is God's purpose for the earth?

"God blessed them and God said to them: 'Be fruitful and become many and fill the earth and subdue it, and have in subjection the fish of the sea and the flying creatures of the heavens and every living creature that is moving upon the earth.'" (Gen. 1:28) "Jehovah . . . the Creator of the heavens, He the true God, the Former of the earth and the Maker of it, He the One who firmly established it, . . . did not create it simply for nothing, [he] formed it even to be inhabited." (Isa. 45:18) "As regards the heavens, to Jehovah the heavens belong, but the earth he has given to the sons of men." (Ps. 115:16) "Let your kingdom come. Let your will take place, as in heaven, also upon earth." (Matt. 6:10)

How will this purpose be realized?

"In the days of those kings the God of heaven will set up a kingdom that will never be brought to ruin. And the kingdom itself will not be passed on to any other people. It will crush and put an end to all these kingdoms, and it itself will stand to times indefinite." (Dan. 2:44) "Evildoers themselves will be cut off, but those hoping in Jehovah are the ones that will possess the earth. And just a little while longer, and the wicked one will be no more; and you will certainly give attention to his place, and he will not be. But the meek ones themselves will possess the earth, and they will indeed find their exquisite delight in the abundance of peace. The righteous themselves will possess the earth, and they will reside forever upon it." (Ps. 37:9-11, 29)

What conditions will prevail on earth in God's new system of things?

"There are new heavens and a new earth that we are awaiting according to his promise, and in these righteousness is to dwell." (2 Pet. 3:13) "I saw a new heaven and a new earth; for the former heaven and the former earth had passed away, and the sea is no more. I saw also the holy city, New Jerusalem, coming down out of heaven from God and prepared as a bride adorned for her husband. With that I heard a loud voice from the throne say: 'Look! the tent of God is with mankind, and he will reside with them, and they will be his peoples. And God himself will be with them. And he will wipe out every tear from their eyes, and death will be no more, neither will mourning nor outcry nor pain be any more. The former things have passed away.'" (Rev. 21:1-4) "'They will certainly build houses and have occupancy; and they will certainly plant vineyards and eat their fruitage. They will not build and someone else have occupancy; they will not plant and someone else do the eating. For like the days of a tree will the days of my people be; and the work of their own hands my chosen ones will use to the full. They will not toil for nothing, nor will they bring to birth for disturbance; because they are the offspring made up of the chosen ones of Jehovah, and their descendants with them. And it will actually occur that before they call out I myself shall answer; while they are yet speaking, I myself shall hear. The wolf and the lamb themselves will feed as one, and the lion will eat straw just like the bull; and as for the serpent, his food will be dust. They will do no harm nor cause any ruin in all my holy mountain,' Jehovah has said." (Isa. 65:21-25) "There must go forth a twig out of the stump of Jesse; and out of his roots a sprout will be fruitful. And upon him the spirit of Jehovah must settle down, the spirit of wisdom and of understanding, the spirit of counsel and of mightiness, the spirit of knowledge and of the fear of Jehovah; and there will be enjoyment by him in the fear of Jehovah. And he will not judge by any mere appearance to his eyes, nor reprove simply according to the thing heard by his ears. And with righteousness he must judge the lowly ones, and with uprightness he must give reproof in behalf of the meek ones of the earth. And he must strike the earth with the rod of his mouth; and with the spirit of his lips he will put the wicked one to death. And righteousness must prove to be the belt of his hips, and faithfulness the belt of his loins. And the wolf will actually reside for a while with the male lamb, and with the kid the leopard itself will lie down, and the calf and the maned young lion and the well-fed animal all together; and a mere little boy will be leader over them. And the cow and the bear themselves will feed; together their young ones will lie down. And even the lion will eat straw just like the bull. And the sucking child will certainly play upon the hole of the cobra; and upon the light aperture of a poisonous snake will a weaned child actually put his own hand. They will not do any harm or cause any ruin in all my holy mountain; because the earth will certainly be filled with the knowledge of Jehovah as the waters are covering the very sea." (Isa. 11:1-9) "He will actually swallow up death forever, and the Lord Jehovah will certainly wipe the tears from all faces. And the reproach of his people he will take away from all the earth, for Jehovah himself has spoken it." (Isa. 25:8) "The earth itself will certainly give its produce; God, our God, will bless us." (Ps. 67:6) "Come, you people, behold the activities of Jehovah, how he has set astonishing events on the earth. He is making wars to cease to the extremity of the earth. The bow he breaks apart and does cut the spear in pieces; the wagons he burns in the fire." (Ps. 46:8, 9)

What is the urgent work that the Bible sets out for all Christians at this time?

"This good news of the kingdom will be preached in all the inhabited earth for a witness to all the nations; and then the end will come." (Matt. 24:14) "Go therefore and make disciples of people of all the nations, baptizing them in the name of the Father and of the Son and of the holy spirit, teaching them to observe all the things I have commanded you. And, look! I am with you all the days until the conclusion of the system of things." (Matt. 28:19, 20) "Through him let us always offer to God a sacrifice of praise, that is, the fruit of lips which make public declaration to his name." (Heb. 13:15)

In what manner is this work to be done?

"I did not hold back from telling you any of the things that were profitable nor from teaching you publicly and from house to house." (Acts 20:20) "According to Paul's custom . . . he reasoned with them from the Scriptures." (Acts 17:2) "Preach the word, be at it urgently." (2 Tim. 4:2) "Now Jesus, tired out from the journey, was sitting at the fountain just as he was. The hour was about the sixth. A woman of Samaria came to draw water. . . . Jesus said to her: 'Everyone drinking from this water will get thirsty again. Whoever drinks from the water that I will give him will never get thirsty at all, but the water that I will give him will become in him a fountain of water bubbling up to impart everlasting life.' The woman said to him: 'Sir, give me this water, so that I may neither thirst nor keep coming over to this place to draw water.' " (John

4:6-15) [Overseer will outline arrangements congregation has made to assist all to share in the field ministry
at times that fit their personal circumstances.]

Is this work done in our own strength?

"We have this treasure in earthen vessels, that the
power beyond what is normal may be God's and not
that out of ourselves." (2 Cor. 4:7) "For all things I
have the strength by virtue of him who imparts power
to me." (Phil. 4:13) "The Lord stood near me and in-
fused power into me, that through me the preaching
might be fully accomplished and all the nations might
hear it." (2 Tim. 4:17)

Why are Christians called Jehovah's witnesses?

" 'You are my witnesses,' is the utterance of Jehovah,
'even my servant whom I have chosen, in order that
you may know and have faith in me, and that you may
understand that I am the same One. Before me there
was no God formed, and after me there continued to
be none. I—I am Jehovah, and besides me there is no
savior. I myself have told forth and have saved and
have caused it to be heard, when there was among you
no strange god. So you are my witnesses,' is the
utterance of Jehovah, 'and I am God.' " (Isa. 43:10-12)
"Jesus Christ, 'the Faithful Witness,' 'The first-born
from the dead,' and 'The Ruler of the kings of the
earth.' " (Rev. 1:5)

Who or what is the "faithful and discreet slave"?

" 'Have no fear, *little flock*, because your Father has
approved of giving you the kingdom. Let your loins
be girded and your lamps be burning, and you yourselves be like men waiting for their master when he
returns from the marriage, so that at his arriving and
knocking they may at once open to him. Happy are
those slaves whom the master on arriving finds watch-
ing! . . . You also, keep ready, because at an hour that
you do not think likely the Son of man is coming.' Then
Peter said: 'Lord, are you saying this illustration to us
or also to all?' And the Lord said: 'Who really is the
faithful steward, the discreet one, whom his master will
appoint over his body of attendants to keep giving them
their measure of food supplies at the proper time?
Happy is that slave, if his master on arriving finds him

doing so! I tell you truthfully, He will appoint him over all his belongings.'" (Luke 12:32, 35-44; see also Matthew 24:45-47.) "You are my witnesses, . . . my servant." (Isa. 43:10)

Why is it beneficial to attend the meetings arranged by the congregation?

"Let us consider one another to incite to love and fine works, not forsaking the gathering of ourselves together, as some have the custom, but encouraging one another, and all the more so as you behold the day drawing near." (Heb. 10:24, 25) "One isolating himself will seek his own selfish longing; against all practical wisdom he will break forth." (Prov. 18:1) "I am longing to see you, . . . that there may be an interchange of encouragement among you, by each one through the other's faith, both yours and mine." (Rom. 1:11, 12)

Why is personal study important in the life of a Christian?

"Now the latter were more noble-minded than those in Thessalonica, for they received the word with the greatest eagerness of mind, carefully examining the Scriptures daily as to whether these things were so." (Acts 17:11) "This book of the law should not depart from your mouth, and you must in an undertone read in it day and night, in order that you may take care to do according to all that is written in it; for then you will make your way successful and then you will act wisely." (Josh. 1:8)

Who is the Devil? What is his origin?

"Now the serpent proved to be the most cautious of all the wild beasts of the field that Jehovah God had made. So it began to say to the woman: 'Is it really so that God said you must not eat from every tree of the garden?' At this the woman said to the serpent: 'Of the fruit of the trees of the garden we may eat. But as for eating of the fruit of the tree that is in the middle of the garden, God has said, "You must not eat from it, no, you must not touch it that you do not die." ' At this the serpent said to the woman: 'You positively will not die. For God knows that in the very day of your eating from it your eyes are bound to be opened and you are bound to be like God, knowing good and bad.'" (Gen. 3:1-5) "So down the great dragon was hurled, the original serpent, the one called Devil and Satan, who is misleading the entire inhabited earth; he was hurled down to the earth, and his angels were hurled down with him." (Rev. 12:9) "Put on the complete suit of armor from God that you may be able to stand firm against the machinations of the Devil; because we have a fight, not against blood and flesh, but . . . against the wicked spirit forces in the heavenly places." (Eph. 6:11, 12)

Against what spiritistic practices employed by the Devil and his demons does the Bible warn us?

"There should not be found in you anyone who makes his son or his daughter pass through the fire, anyone who employs divination, a practicer of magic or anyone who looks for omens or a sorcerer, or one who binds others with a spell or anyone who consults a spirit medium or a professional foreteller of events or anyone who inquires of the dead." (Deut. 18:10, 11) "As we were going to the place of prayer, a certain servant girl with a spirit, a demon of divination, met us. She used to furnish her masters with much gain by practicing the art of prediction." (Acts 16:16) [List practices that are prevalent in your locality.]

How can we protect ourselves against the influence of these wicked spirits?

"Subject yourselves, therefore, to God; but oppose the Devil, and he will flee from you." (Jas. 4:7) "Put on the complete suit of armor from God that you may be able to stand firm against the machinations of the Devil . . . On this account take up the complete suit of armor from God, that you may be able to resist in the wicked day and, after you have done all things thoroughly, to stand firm. Stand firm, therefore, with your loins girded about with truth, and having on the breastplate of righteousness, and with your feet shod with the equipment of the good news of peace. Above all things, take up the large shield of faith, with which you will be able to quench all the wicked one's burning missiles. Also, accept the helmet of salvation, and the sword of the spirit, that is, God's word, while with every form of prayer and supplication you carry on prayer on every occasion in spirit." (Eph. 6:11-18)

Why has God permitted wickedness to continue until now?

"What shall we say, then? Is there injustice with God? Never may that become so! For he says to Moses: 'I will have mercy upon whomever I do have mercy, and I will show compassion to whomever I do show compassion.' So, then, it depends, not upon the one wishing nor upon the one running, but upon God, who has mercy. For the Scripture says to Pharaoh: 'For this very cause I have let you remain, that in connection with you I may show my power, and that my name may be declared in all the earth.' So, then, upon whom he wishes he has mercy, but whom he wishes he lets become obstinate. . . . God, although having the will to demonstrate his wrath and to make his power known, tolerated with much long-suffering vessels of wrath made fit for destruction, in order that he might make known the riches of his glory upon vessels of mercy, which he prepared beforehand for glory." (Rom. 9:14-23; see also Job 1:9-12; 2:4-6.) "Jehovah is not slow respecting his promise, as some people consider slowness, but he is patient with you because he does not desire any to be destroyed but desires all to attain to repentance. Furthermore, consider the patience of our Lord as salvation, just as our beloved brother Paul according to the wisdom given him also wrote you." (2 Pet. 3:9, 15)

By what means will God destroy the wicked?

"He cried out with a strong voice, saying: 'She has fallen! Babylon the great has fallen, and she has become a dwelling place of demons and a lurking place of every unclean exhalation and a lurking place of every unclean and hated bird! For because of the passion-arousing wine of her fornication all the nations have fallen victim, and the kings of the earth committed fornication with her, and the traveling merchants of the earth became rich due to the power of her shameless luxury.' . . . 'For her sins have massed together clear up to heaven, and God has called her acts of injustice to mind. That is why in one day her plagues will come, death and mourning and famine, and she will be completely burned with fire, because Jehovah God, who judged her, is strong.'" (Rev. 18: 2-5, 8) "I saw the heaven opened, and, look! a white horse. And the one seated upon it is called Faithful and

True, and he judges and carries on war in righteousness. And out of his mouth there protrudes a sharp long sword, that he may strike the nations with it, and he will shepherd them with a rod of iron. He treads too the press of the wine of the anger of the wrath of God the Almighty. And I saw the wild beast and the kings of the earth and their armies gathered together to wage the war with the one seated on the horse and with his army. And the wild beast was caught, and along with it the false prophet that performed in front of it the signs with which he misled those who received the mark of the wild beast and those who render worship to its image. While still alive, they both were hurled into the fiery lake that burns with sulphur. But the rest were killed off with the long sword of the one seated on the horse, which sword proceeded out of his mouth. And all the birds were filled from the fleshy parts of them." (Rev. 19:11, 15, 19-21) "I saw an angel coming down out of heaven with the key of the abyss and a great chain in his hand. And he seized the dragon, the original serpent, who is the Devil and Satan, and bound him for a thousand years. And he hurled him into the abyss and shut it and sealed it over him, that he might not mislead the nations any more until the thousand years were ended. After these things he must be let loose for a little while. Now as soon as the thousand years have been ended, Satan will be let loose out of his prison, and he will go out to mislead those nations in the four corners of the earth, Gog and Magog, to gather them together for the war. The number of these is as the sand of the sea. And the Devil who was misleading them was hurled into the lake of fire and sulphur, where both the wild beast and the false prophet already were." (Rev. 20:1-3, 7, 8, 10)

What is the human soul? Can it die?

"Jehovah God proceeded to form the man out of dust from the ground and to blow into his nostrils the breath of life, and the man came to be a living soul." (Gen. 2:7; see also 1 Corinthians 15:45.) "Look! All the souls—to me they belong. As the soul of the father so likewise the soul of the son—to me they belong. The soul that is sinning—it itself will die." (Ezek. 18:4) "Indeed, any soul that does not listen to that Prophet will be completely destroyed from among the people." (Acts 3:23)

What is sin?

"Everyone who practices sin is also practicing law-lessness, and so sin is lawlessness." (1 John 3:4) "All have sinned and fall short of the glory of God." (Rom. 3:23)

How did we all become sinners?

"Through one man sin entered into the world and death through sin, and thus death spread to all men because they had all sinned." (Rom. 5:12)

Is there any human who is not a sinner?

"If we make the statement: 'We have no sin,' we are misleading ourselves and the truth is not in us." (1 John 1:8) "There is no man that does not sin." (1 Ki. 8:46)

What should be our attitude toward the committing of sins?

"Do not let sin continue to rule as king in your mortal bodies that you should obey their desires. Neither go on presenting your members to sin as weapons of unrighteousness, but present yourselves to God as those alive from the dead, also your members to God as weapons of righteousness. For sin must not be master over you, seeing that you are not under law but under undeserved kindness." (Rom. 6:12-14)

What is death?

"He said to them: 'Lazarus our friend has gone to rest, but I am journeying there to awaken him from sleep.' Therefore the disciples said to him: 'Lord, if he has gone to rest, he will get well.' Jesus had spoken, however, about his death. But they imagined he was speaking about taking rest in sleep. At that time, therefore, Jesus said to them outspokenly: 'Lazarus has died.'" (John 11:11-14) "The living are conscious that they will die; but as for the dead, they are conscious of nothing at all, neither do they any more have wages, because the remembrance of them has been forgotten. All that your hand finds to do, do with your very power, for there is no work nor devising nor knowledge nor wisdom in Sheol, the place to which you are going." (Eccl. 9:5, 10) "In the sweat of your face you will eat bread until you return to the ground, for out of it you were taken. For dust you are and to dust you will return." (Gen. 3:19)

Why do people die?

"The wages sin pays is death." (Rom. 6:23) "In Adam all are dying." (1 Cor. 15:22)

What future hope for life is there for one who dies?

"I have hope toward God, which hope these men themselves also entertain, that there is going to be a resurrection of both the righteous and the unrighteous." (Acts 24:15) "Do not marvel at this, because the hour is coming in which all those in the memorial tombs will hear his voice and come out, those who did good things to a resurrection of life, those who practiced vile things to a resurrection of judgment." (John 5:28, 29) "The sea gave up those dead in it, and death and Hades gave up those dead in them, and they were judged individually according to their deeds." (Rev. 20:13)

How many from among mankind will be in heaven with Christ?

"I saw, and, look! the Lamb standing upon the Mount Zion, and with him a hundred and forty-four thousand having his name and the name of his Father written on their foreheads. And they are singing as if a new song before the throne and before the four living creatures and the older persons; and no one was able to master that song but the hundred and forty-four thousand, who have been bought from the earth." (Rev. 14:1, 3; see also 7:4-8.)

What will they do there?

"You made them to be a kingdom and priests to our God, and they will rule as kings over the earth." (Rev. 5:10) "I saw thrones, and there were those who sat down on them, and power of judging was given them. Yes, I saw the souls of those executed with the ax for the witness they bore to Jesus and for speaking about God, and those who had worshiped neither the wild beast nor its image and who had not received the mark upon their forehead and upon their hand. And they came to life and ruled as kings with the Christ for a thousand years. Happy and holy is anyone having part in the first resurrection; over these the second

death has no authority, but they will be priests of God
and of the Christ, and will rule as kings with him for a
thousand years." (Rev. 20:4, 6)

Are Christians under the law covenant with its requirements of sabbath keeping and sacrifice?

"Christ is the end of the Law, so that everyone exercising faith may have righteousness." (Rom. 10:4) "The
Law has become our tutor leading to Christ, that we
might be declared righteous due to faith. But now that
the faith has arrived, we are no longer under a tutor."
(Gal. 3:24, 25) "Therefore let no man judge you in
eating and drinking or in respect of a festival or of an
observance of the new moon or of a sabbath; for those
things are a shadow of the things to come, but the
reality belongs to the Christ." (Col. 2:16, 17)

Why must lying be avoided?

"The Devil . . . did not stand fast in the truth, because
truth is not in him. When he speaks the lie, he speaks
according to his own disposition, because he is a liar
and the father of the lie." (John 8:44) "There are six
things that Jehovah does hate; yes, seven are things
detestable to his soul: lofty eyes, a false tongue, and
hands that are shedding innocent blood, a heart
fabricating hurtful schemes, feet that are in a hurry to
run to badness, a false witness that launches forth lies,
and anyone sending forth contentions among brothers."
(Prov. 6:16-19) "As for . . . all the liars, their portion
will be in the lake that burns with fire and sulphur.
This means the second death." (Rev. 21:8)

What is the Christian view of stealing?

"Let none of you suffer as a murderer or a thief or
an evildoer or as a busybody in other people's matters."
(1 Pet. 4:15) "Let the stealer steal no more, but rather
let him do hard work, doing with his hands what is
good work, that he may have something to distribute to
someone in need." (Eph. 4:28)

What is the Christian view of drunkenness?

"What! Do you not know that unrighteous persons
will not inherit God's kingdom? Do not be misled.
Neither fornicators, nor idolaters, nor adulterers, . . .
nor greedy persons, nor drunkards . . . will inherit God's
kingdom." (1 Cor. 6:9, 10) "Ministerial servants should

likewise be serious, . . . not giving themselves to a lot of wine." (1 Tim. 3:8)

What is God's law concerning blood?

"Every moving animal that is alive may serve as food for you. As in the case of green vegetation, I do give it all for you. Only flesh with its soul—its blood—you must not eat." (Gen. 9:3, 4; see also Deuteronomy 12:15, 16.) "The holy spirit and we ourselves have favored adding no further burden to you, except these necessary things, to keep yourselves free from things sacrificed to idols and from blood and from things strangled and from fornication. If you carefully keep yourselves from these things, you will prosper. Good health to you!" (Acts 15:28, 29) [List local practices that are affected by this law.]

What does the Bible say about such practices as fornication, adultery and sexual relations with another person of the same sex? May a person who is engaging in such practices be baptized?

"Now the works of the flesh are manifest, and they are fornication, uncleanness, loose conduct, idolatry, practice of spiritism, hatreds, strife, jealousy, fits of anger, contentions, divisions, sects, envies, drunken bouts, revelries, and things like these. As to these things I am forewarning you, the same way as I did forewarn you, that those who practice such things will not inherit God's kingdom." (Gal. 5:19-21) "Let marriage be honorable among all, and the marriage bed be without defilement, for God will judge fornicators and adulterers." (Heb. 13:4) "Therefore God, in keeping with the desires of their hearts, gave them up to uncleanness, that their bodies might be dishonored among them, even those who exchanged the truth of God for the lie and venerated and rendered sacred service to the creation rather than the One who created, who is blessed forever. Amen. That is why God gave them up to disgraceful sexual appetites, for both their females changed the natural use of themselves into one contrary to nature; and likewise even the males left the natural use of the female and became violently inflamed in their lust toward one another, males with males, working what is obscene and receiving in themselves the full recompense, which was due for their error." (Rom. 1:24-27) "Deaden, therefore, your body members that are upon the earth as respects fornication, uncleanness, sexual appetite, hurtful desire, and covetousness, which is idolatry. On account of those things the wrath of God is coming. In those very things you, too, once walked when you used to live in them. But now really put them all away from you, wrath, anger, injuriousness, abusive speech, and obscene talk out of your mouth. Do not be lying to one another. Strip off the old personality with its practices, and clothe yourselves with the new personality, which through accurate knowledge is being made new according to the image of the One who created it." (Col. 3:5-10) "This, therefore, I say and bear witness to in the Lord, that you no longer go on walking just as the nations also walk in the unprofitableness of their minds, while they are in darkness mentally, and alienated from the life that belongs to God, because of the ignorance that is in them, because of the insensibility of their hearts. Having come to be past all moral sense, they gave themselves over to loose conduct to work uncleanness of every sort with greediness. But you did not learn the Christ to be so, provided, indeed, that you heard him and were taught by means of him, just as truth is in Jesus, that you should put away the old personality which conforms to your former course of conduct and which is being corrupted according to his deceptive desires; but that you should be made new in the force actuating your mind, and should put on the new personality which was created according to God's will in true righteousness and loyalty." (Eph. 4:17-24)

Why is moral cleanness of all persons in Jehovah's organization important to every one of us?

"Many will follow their acts of loose conduct, and on account of these the way of the truth will be spoken of abusively." (2 Pet. 2:2) "Beloved ones, though I was making every effort to write you about the salvation we hold in common, I found it necessary to write you to exhort you to put up a hard fight for the faith that was once for all time delivered to the holy ones. My reason is that certain men have slipped in who have long ago been appointed by the Scriptures to this judgment, ungodly men, turning the undeserved kindness of our God into an excuse for loose conduct and proving

false to our only Owner and Lord, Jesus Christ."
(Jude 3, 4; see also Joshua 7:1-26.)

**What action does the congregation take when a person in
its midst proves himself to be a persistent and unrepentant violator of God's commandments?**

"In my letter I wrote you to quit mixing in company
with fornicators, not meaning entirely with the fornicators of this world or the greedy persons and extortioners or idolaters. Otherwise, you would actually have
to get out of the world. But now I am writing you to
quit mixing in company with anyone called a brother
that is a fornicator or a greedy person or an idolater
or a reviler or a drunkard or an extortioner, not even
eating with such a man. For what do I have to do with
judging those outside? Do you not judge those inside,
while God judges those outside? 'Remove the wicked
man from among yourselves.'" (1 Cor. 5:9-13)

**If a person in weakness commits a serious sin, but he
wants help to be restored to Jehovah's favor, what action
should he take?**

"Let him call the older men of the congregation to
him, and let them pray over him, greasing him with oil
in the name of Jehovah. And the prayer of faith will
make the indisposed one well, and Jehovah will raise
him up. Also, if he has committed sins, it will be forgiven him." (Jas. 5:14, 15) "Brothers, even though a
man takes some false step before he is aware of it, you
who have spiritual qualifications try to restore such a
man in a spirit of mildness, as you each keep an eye on
yourself, for fear you also may be tempted." (Gal. 6:1)
"He that is covering over his transgressions will not
succeed, but he that is confessing and leaving them will
be shown mercy." (Prov. 28:13) "My sin I finally confessed to you, and my error I did not cover. I said: 'I
shall make confession over my transgressions to Jehovah.' And you yourself pardoned the error of my sins."
(Ps. 32:5) "My little children, I am writing you these
things that you may not commit a sin. And yet, if anyone does commit a sin, we have a helper with the
Father, Jesus Christ, a righteous one. And he is a
propitiatory sacrifice for our sins, yet not for ours only
but also for the whole world's." (1 John 2:1, 2)

What Christian quality should outstandingly characterize our relationship with our spiritual brothers and with the members of our own families?

"I am giving you a new commandment, that you love one another; just as I have loved you, that you also love one another. By this all will know that you are my disciples, if you have love among yourselves." (John 13:34, 35) "Husbands, continue loving your wives, just as the Christ also loved the congregation and delivered up himself for it." (Eph. 5:25) "Recall the young women to their senses to love their husbands, to love their children." (Titus 2:4) "Continue putting up with one another and forgiving one another freely if anyone has a cause for complaint against another. Even as Jehovah freely forgave you, so do you also. But, besides all these things, clothe yourselves with love, for it is a perfect bond of union." (Col. 3:13, 14)

In God's arrangement of things, who is the head of a married woman?

"You wives, be in subjection to your husbands, as it is becoming in the Lord." (Col. 3:18) "Let wives be in subjection to their husbands as to the Lord, because a husband is head of his wife as the Christ also is head of the congregation, he being a savior of this body." (Eph. 5:22, 23)

Is the wife whose husband is not a believer freed from his headship?

"You wives, be in subjection to your own husbands, in order that, if any are not obedient to the word, they may be won without a word through the conduct of their wives, because of having been eyewitnesses of your chaste conduct together with deep respect." (1 Pet. 3:1, 2) "A married woman is bound by law to her husband while he is alive; but if her husband dies, she is discharged from the law of her husband." (Rom. 7:2)

Who is responsible before God for the training and disciplining of children?

"You, fathers, do not be irritating your children, but go on bringing them up in the discipline and authoritative advice of Jehovah." (Eph. 6:4) "The one holding back his rod is hating his son, but the one loving him is he that does look for him with discipline." (Prov. 13:

24) "The rod and reproof are what give wisdom; but a boy let on the loose will be causing his mother shame." (Prov. 29:15)

May a Christian have more than one living marriage mate?

"The overseer should therefore be irreprehensible, a husband of one wife." (1 Tim. 3:2) " 'A man will leave his father and his mother and will stick to his wife, and the two will be one flesh' . . . So that they are no longer two, but one flesh." (Matt. 19:5, 6)

What is the only Scriptural basis for divorce that frees one to remarry?

"I say to you that whoever divorces his wife, except on the ground of fornication, and marries another commits adultery." (Matt. 19:9) "Everyone divorcing his wife, except on account of fornication, makes her a subject for adultery, seeing that whoever marries a divorced woman commits adultery." (Matt. 5:32)

Is it necessary for persons who are living together as husband and wife to have their marriage legally registered with the government?

"Let marriage be honorable among all, and the marriage bed be without defilement, for God will judge fornicators and adulterers." (Heb. 13:4) "Continue reminding them to be in subjection and be obedient to governments and authorities as rulers, to be ready for every good work." (Titus 3:1) "Now in those days a decree went forth . . . for all the inhabited earth to be registered . . . Of course, Joseph also went up from Galilee . . . to get registered with Mary, who had been given him in marriage." (Luke 2:1-5)

What is the fruitage of the spirit?

"The fruitage of the spirit is love, joy, peace, longsuffering, kindness, goodness, faith, mildness, self-control." (Gal. 5:22, 23)

Is it reasonable to expect a Christian to manifest this fruitage in his life?

"Keep walking by spirit and you will carry out no fleshly desire at all. If we are living by spirit, let us go on walking orderly also by spirit." (Gal. 5:16, 25)

Does that mean that we will be able to do this perfectly?

"Brothers, even though a man takes some false step before he is aware of it, you who have spiritual qualifications try to restore such a man in a spirit of mildness, as you each keep an eye on yourself, for fear you also may be tempted." (Gal. 6:1)

How should Christians view the shortcomings of fellow believers?

"Stop judging that you may not be judged; for with what judgment you are judging, you will be judged; and with the measure that you are measuring out, they will measure out to you. Why, then, do you look at the straw in your brother's eye, but do not consider the rafter in your own eye? Or how can you say to your brother, 'Allow me to extract the straw from your eye'; when, look! a rafter is in your own eye? Hypocrite! First extract the rafter from your own eye, and then you will see clearly how to extract the straw from your brother's eye." (Matt. 7:1-5) "Let us not be judging one another any longer, but rather make this your decision, not to put before a brother a stumbling block or a cause for tripping. . . . So, then, let us pursue the things making for peace and the things that are upbuilding to one another." (Rom. 14:13-19)

When personal difficulties arise between individuals, what is the Christian way to correct the situation?

"If your brother commits a sin, go lay bare his fault between you and him alone. If he listens to you, you have gained your brother. But if he does not listen, take along with you one or two more, in order that at the mouth of two or three witnesses every matter may be established. If he does not listen to them, speak to the congregation. If he does not listen even to the congregation, let him be to you just as a man of the nations and as a tax collector." (Matt. 18:15-17; see also verses 21-35.)

What does the Bible say about sharing with other religious groups in worship or any of the other activities in which they engage?

"Do not become unevenly yoked with unbelievers. For what sharing do righteousness and lawlessness have? Or what fellowship does light have with darkness? Further, what harmony is there between Christ and Belial? Or what portion does a faithful person have with an unbeliever? And what agreement does God's temple have with idols? For we are a temple of a living God; just as God said: 'I shall reside among them and walk among them, and I shall be their God, and they will be my people.' ' "Therefore get out from among them, and separate yourselves," says Jehovah, "and quit touching the unclean thing" '; ' "and I will take you in." ' ' "And I shall be a father to you, and you will be sons and daughters to me," says Jehovah the Almighty.' " (2 Cor. 6:14-18) "I heard another voice out of heaven say: 'Get out of her, my people, if you do not want to share with her in her sins, and if you do not want to receive part of her plagues. For her sins have massed together clear up to heaven, and God has called her acts of injustice to mind.' " (Rev. 18:4, 5) "The things which the nations sacrifice they sacrifice to demons, and not to God; and I do not want you to become sharers with the demons." (1 Cor. 10:20) "Go in through the narrow gate; because broad and spacious is the road leading off into destruction, and many are the ones going in through it; whereas narrow is the gate and cramped the road leading off into life, and few are the ones finding it. Not everyone saying to me, 'Lord, Lord,' will enter into the kingdom of the heavens, but the one doing the will of my Father who is in the heavens will. Many will say to me in that day, 'Lord, Lord, did we not prophesy in your name, and expel demons in your name, and perform many powerful works in your name?' And yet then I will confess to them: I never knew you! Get away from me, you workers of lawlessness." (Matt. 7:13, 14, 21-23) "Men will be . . . having a form of godly devotion but proving false to its power; and from these turn away." (2 Tim. 3:2, 5) [Consider changes that this may necessitate in one's life.]

What is the only religious celebration that Christians are commanded to observe?

"I received from the Lord that which I also handed on to you, that the Lord Jesus in the night in which he was going to be handed over took a loaf and, after giving thanks, he broke it and said: 'This means my body which is in your behalf. Keep doing this in remembrance of me.' He did likewise respecting the cup also, after he had the evening meal, saying: 'This cup means the new covenant by virtue of my blood. Keep doing this, as often as you drink it, in remembrance of me.' For as often as you eat this loaf and drink this cup, you keep proclaiming the death of the Lord, until he arrives." (1 Cor. 11:23-26)

What Bible principles should guide us in determining whether other celebrations that are popular in the community are acceptable for Christians?

"They are no part of the world, just as I am no part of the world." (John 17:16) "Do not be loving either the world or the things in the world. If anyone loves the world, the love of the Father is not in him; because everything in the world—the desire of the flesh and the desire of the eyes and the showy display of one's means of life—does not originate with the Father, but originates with the world. Furthermore, the world is passing away and so is its desire, but he that does the will of God remains forever." (1 John 2:15-17) "When Herod's birthday was being celebrated the daughter of Herodias danced at it and pleased Herod so much that he promised with an oath to give her whatever she asked. Then she, under her mother's coaching, said: 'Give me here upon a platter the head of John the Baptist.' Grieved though he was, the king out of regard for his oaths and for those reclining with him commanded it to be given; and he sent and had John beheaded in the prison." (Matt. 14:6-10) "The time that has passed by is sufficient for you to have worked out the will of the nations when you proceeded in deeds of loose conduct, lusts, excesses with wine, revelries, drinking matches, and illegal idolatries." (1 Pet. 4:3) "What sharing do righteousness and lawlessness have? Or what fellowship does light have with darkness? Further, what harmony is there between Christ and Belial? Or what portion does a faithful person have with an unbeliever? And what agreement does God's temple have with idols? . . . '"Therefore get out from among them, and separate yourselves," says Jehovah, "and quit touching the unclean thing"'; '"and I will take you in."'" (2 Cor. 6:14-17) [Analyze application of these scriptures to activities that are popular in your area.]

Whom does the Bible identify as the "ruler of the world" and "the god of this system of things"?

"I shall not speak much with you any more, for the ruler of the world is coming. And he has no hold on me [Jesus Christ]." (John 14:30) "We know we originate with God, but the whole world is lying in the power of the wicked one." (1 John 5:19) "The god of this system of things has blinded the minds of the unbelievers, that the illumination of the glorious good news about the Christ, who is the image of God, might not shine through." (2 Cor. 4:4) "Down the great dragon was hurled, the original serpent, the one called Devil and Satan, who is misleading the entire inhabited earth; he was hurled down to the earth, and his angels were hurled down with him." (Rev. 12:9)

What is the position of Christians as to this world?

"If you were part of the world, the world would be fond of what is its own. Now because you are no part of the world, but I have chosen you out of the world, on this account the world hates you." (John 15:19) "I request you, not to take them out of the world, but to watch over them because of the wicked one. They are no part of the world, just as I am no part of the world." (John 17:15, 16) "Do you not know that the friendship with the world is enmity with God? Whoever, therefore, wants to be a friend of the world is constituting himself an enemy of God." (Jas. 4:4)

What was Jesus' attitude toward all participation in the political affairs of the world?

"The Devil took him along to an unusually high mountain, and showed him all the kingdoms of the world and their glory, and he said to him: 'All these things I will give you if you fall down and do an act of worship to me.' Then Jesus said to him: 'Go away, Satan! For it is written, "It is Jehovah your God you must worship, and it is to him alone you must render sacred service." ' " (Matt. 4:8-10) "Jesus, knowing they were about to come and seize him to make him king, withdrew again into the mountain all alone." (John 6:15) "Jesus answered: 'My kingdom is no part of this world. If my kingdom were part of this world, my attendants would have fought that I should not be delivered up to the Jews. But, as it is, my kingdom is

not from this source.' " (John 18:36) [Consider the
application of these texts to situations that arise in
your locality.]

How do Bible commands concerning idolatry affect a Christian in this modern world?

"Guard yourselves from idols." (1 John 5:21) "You
must not make for yourself a carved image or a form
like anything that is in the heavens above or that is on
the earth underneath or that is in the waters under the
earth. You must not bow down to them nor be induced
to serve them, because I Jehovah your God am a God
exacting exclusive devotion." (Ex. 20:4, 5) "I am Jehovah. That is my name; and to no one else shall I give
my own glory, neither my praise to graven images."
(Isa. 42:8) "Their idols are silver and gold, the work
of the hands of earthling man. A mouth they have,
but they cannot speak; eyes they have, but they cannot
see; ears they have, but they cannot hear. A nose they
have, but they cannot smell. Hands are theirs, but they
cannot feel. Feet are theirs, but they cannot walk; they
utter no sound with their throat. Those making them
will become just like them, all those who are trusting
in them." (Ps. 115:4-8) "Nebuchadnezzar the king made
an image of gold, the height of which was sixty cubits
and the breadth of which was six cubits. He set it up
in the plain of Dura in the jurisdictional district of
Babylon. . . . And the herald was crying out loudly: 'To
you it is being said, O peoples, national groups and
languages, that at the time that you hear the sound
of the horn, the pipe, the zither, the triangular harp,
the stringed instrument, the bagpipe and all sorts of
musical instruments, you fall down and worship the
image of gold that Nebuchadnezzar the king has set
up. And whoever does not fall down and worship will
at the same moment be thrown into the burning fiery
furnace.' . . . Shadrach, Meshach and Abednego answered, and they were saying to the king: . . . 'But if
not, let it become known to you, O king, that your gods
are not the ones we are serving, and the image of gold
that you have set up we will not worship.' " (Dan. 3:
1-18) "On a set day Herod clothed himself with royal
raiment and sat down upon the judgment seat and
began giving them a public address. In turn the assembled people began shouting: 'A god's voice, and not

a man's!' Instantly the angel of Jehovah struck him, because he did not give the glory to God; and he became eaten up with worms and expired." (Acts 12:21-23) "If anyone worships the wild beast and its image, and receives a mark on his forehead or upon his hand, he will also drink of the wine of the anger of God that is poured out undiluted into the cup of his wrath, and he shall be tormented with fire and sulphur in the sight of the holy angels and in the sight of the Lamb. And the smoke of their torment ascends forever and ever, and day and night they have no rest, those who worship the wild beast and its image, and whoever receives the mark of its name. Here is where it means endurance for the holy ones, those who observe the commandments of God and the faith of Jesus." (Rev. 14:9-12) [Give examples of situations calling for application of this counsel.]

In the light of the following texts, what is the position of a true Christian in this world?

"It must occur in the final part of the days that the mountain of the house of Jehovah will become firmly established above the top of the mountains, and it will certainly be lifted up above the hills; and to it all the nations must stream. And many peoples will certainly go and say: 'Come, you people, and let us go up to the mountain of Jehovah, to the house of the God of Jacob; and he will instruct us about his ways, and we will walk in his paths.' For out of Zion law will go forth, and the word of Jehovah out of Jerusalem. And he will certainly render judgment among the nations and set matters straight respecting many peoples. And they will have to beat their swords into plowshares and their spears into pruning shears. Nation will not lift up sword against nation, neither will they learn war any more." (Isa. 2:2-4) "They are no part of the world, just as I am no part of the world." (John 17:16) "Though we walk in the flesh, we do not wage warfare according to what we are in the flesh. For the weapons of our warfare are not fleshly, but powerful by God for overturning strongly entrenched things." (2 Cor. 10:3, 4) "Do not you people be owing anybody a single thing, except to love one another; for he that loves his fellow man has fulfilled the law. For the law code, 'You must not commit adultery, You must not murder,

You must not steal, You must not covet,' and whatever other commandment there is, is summed up in this word, namely, 'You must love your neighbor as yourself.' Love does not work evil to one's neighbor; therefore love is the law's fulfillment." (Rom. 13:8-10) "Then Jesus said to him: 'Return your sword to its place, for all those who take the sword will perish by the sword.'" (Matt. 26:52) "You were bought with a price; stop becoming slaves of men." (1 Cor. 7:23)

Is it necessary for a Christian to be subject to worldly rulers and to show them respect?

"Let every soul be in subjection to the superior authorities, for there is no authority except by God; the existing authorities stand placed in their relative positions by God. Therefore he who opposes the authority has taken a stand against the arrangement of God; those who have taken a stand against it will receive judgment to themselves. For those ruling are an object of fear, not to the good deed, but to the bad. Do you, then, want to have no fear of the authority? Keep doing good, and you will have praise from it; for it is God's minister to you for your good. But if you are doing what is bad, be in fear: for it is not without purpose that it bears the sword; for it is God's minister, an avenger to express wrath upon the one practicing what is bad. There is therefore compelling reason for you people to be in subjection, not only on account of that wrath but also on account of your conscience. For that is why you are also paying taxes; for they are God's public servants constantly serving this very purpose. Render to all their dues, to him who calls for the tax, the tax; to him who calls for the tribute, the tribute; to him who calls for fear, such fear; to him who calls for honor, such honor." (Rom. 13:1-7) "Continue reminding them to be in subjection and be obedient to governments and authorities as rulers, to be ready for every good work." (Titus 3:1) "Concerning all the things of which I am accused by Jews, King Agrippa, I count myself happy that it is before you I am to make my defense this day, especially as you are expert on all the customs as well as the controversies among Jews. Therefore I beg you to hear me patiently." (Acts 26:2, 3)

Must a Christian pay all the taxes demanded by law?

"They questioned him, saying: 'Teacher, we know you speak and teach correctly and show no partiality, but you teach the way of God in line with truth: Is it lawful for us to pay tax to Caesar or not?' But he detected their cunning and said to them: 'Show me a denarius. Whose image and inscription does it have?' They said: 'Caesar's.' He said to them: 'By all means, then, pay back Caesar's things to Caesar, but God's things to God.'" (Luke 20:21-25) "Render to all their dues, to him who calls for the tax, the tax; to him who calls for the tribute, the tribute; to him who calls for fear, such fear; to him who calls for honor, such honor." (Rom. 13:7)

Is there any circumstance under which a Christian would not obey the law?

"They called them and charged them, nowhere to make any utterance or to teach upon the basis of the name of Jesus. But in reply Peter and John said to them: 'Whether it is righteous in the sight of God to listen to you rather than to God, judge for yourselves. But as for us, we cannot stop speaking about the things we have seen and heard.'" (Acts 4:18-20) "'We positively ordered you not to keep teaching upon the basis of this name, and yet, look! you have filled Jerusalem with your teaching, and you are determined to bring the blood of this man upon us.' In answer Peter and the other apostles said: 'We must obey God as ruler rather than men.'" (Acts 5:28, 29)

Why are true Christians persecuted?

"If you were part of the world, the world would be fond of what is its own. Now because you are no part of the world, but I have chosen you out of the world, on this account the world hates you. Bear in mind the the word I said to you, A slave is not greater than his master. If they have persecuted me, they will persecute you also; if they have observed my word, they will observe yours also. But they will do all these things against you on account of my name, because they do not know him that sent me." (John 15:19-21) "In fact, all those desiring to live with godly devotion in association with Christ Jesus will also be persecuted." (2 Tim. 3:12) "Before all these things people will lay their

hands upon you and persecute you, delivering you up
to the synagogues and prisons, you being haled before
kings and governors for the sake of my name. It will
turn out to you for a witness." (Luke 21:12, 13)

**What are some factors to consider in determining whether
certain types of employment are proper for Christians?**

"Let the stealer steal no more, but rather let him do
hard work, doing with his hands what is good work,
that he may have something to distribute to someone
in need." (Eph. 4:28) "The Devil . . . is a liar and the
father of the lie." (John 8:44) "I heard another voice
out of heaven say: 'Get out of her [Babylon the Great],
my people, if you do not want to share with her in her
sins, and if you do not want to receive part of her
plagues.'" (Rev. 18:4) "What! Do you not know that
unrighteous persons will not inherit God's kingdom? Do
not be misled. Neither fornicators, nor idolaters, nor
adulterers, nor men kept for unnatural purposes, nor
men who lie with men, nor thieves, nor greedy persons,
nor drunkards, nor revilers, nor extortioners will inherit God's kingdom. And yet that is what some of you
were. But you have been washed clean, but you have
been sanctified, but you have been declared righteous in
the name of our Lord Jesus Christ and with the spirit of
our God." (1 Cor. 6:9-11) "'Come, you people, and let
us go up to the mountain of Jehovah and to the house
of the God of Jacob; and he will instruct us about his
ways, and we will walk in his paths.' For out of Zion
law will go forth, and the word of Jehovah out of
Jerusalem. And he will certainly render judgment
among many peoples, and set matters straight respecting mighty nations far away. And they will have
to beat their swords into plowshares and their spears
into pruning shears. They will not lift up sword, nation
against nation, neither will they learn war any more."
(Mic. 4:2, 3) "Write them to abstain . . . from blood."
(Acts 15:20) "Jesus, knowing they were about to come
and seize him to make him king, withdrew again into
the mountain all alone." (John 6:15)

**What should always be our attitude toward the doing
of Jehovah's will?**

"Look! I am come to do your will." (Heb. 10:9)
"Happy is the man in fear of Jehovah, in whose commandments he has taken very much delight." (Ps.

112:1) "You must love Jehovah your God with your whole heart and with your whole soul and with your whole strength and with your whole mind." (Luke 10: 27) "Jesus said to them: 'My food is for me to do the will of him that sent me and to finish his work.'" (John 4:34)

Why should one who has made a dedication to God be baptized?

"Go therefore and make disciples of people of all the nations, baptizing them in the name of the Father and of the Son and of the holy spirit." (Matt. 28:19) "Then Jesus came from Galilee to the Jordan to John, in order to be baptized by him. But the latter tried to prevent him, saying: 'I am the one needing to be baptized by you, and are you coming to me?' In reply Jesus said to him: 'Let it be, this time, for in that way it is suitable for us to carry out all that is righteous.' Then he quit preventing him. After being baptized Jesus immediately came up from the water; and, look! the heavens were opened up, and he saw descending like a dove God's spirit coming upon him. Look! Also, there was a voice from the heavens that said: 'This is my Son, the beloved, whom I have approved.'" (Matt. 3: 13-17) "When they believed Philip, who was declaring the good news of the kingdom of God and of the name of Jesus Christ, they proceeded to be baptized, both men and women." (Acts 8:12) "That which corresponds to this is also now saving you, namely, baptism, (not the putting away of the filth of the flesh, but the request made to God for a good conscience,) through the resurrection of Jesus Christ." (1 Pet. 3:21)

CHAPTER 2

An Organization Based on God's Word

JUST as it is true that God's Word is a lamp to our feet in matters of belief and personal conduct, so, too, it provides organizational instructions. It makes clear to us Jehovah's way of doing things and shows us how we personally can have a share in the carrying out of his purposes.

Therefore, the Holy Bible constitutes the basic organization instructions of Jehovah's Christian witnesses. It contains Jehovah's righteous laws, commandments and judicial decisions. It sets forth principles that must guide our thinking and our actions if we are to be well pleasing to God. What it says applies in every part of the earth and to all persons, without partiality.—Mic. 4:2; Acts 10: 34, 35.

The inspired Word of God informs us that Jehovah has subjected all things to Jesus Christ and has made him the head of the Christian congregation. (Eph. 1:22, 23) At the time of Pentecost, 33 C.E., the glorified Jesus poured out God's holy spirit on his faithful disciples gathered in Jerusalem, in this way designating them, as a class, as his "faithful and discreet slave." (Matt. 24:45) As Jesus had told them in advance, when this happened they were to be witnesses of him, first in Jerusalem and Judea and Samaria, and then to the most distant part of the earth. (Acts 1:8) As new ones were gathered into association with them, those already in the Christian congregation were to supply them with the needed spiritual food. All contributed in various ways to the spiritual upbuilding of the individual members of the congregation.—Eph. 4:16.

Today the remaining ones of Christ's spirit-anointed body members on earth constitute the "faithful and discreet slave," and it is this class, as foretold at Matthew 24:47, that the Lord Jesus has appointed "over *all* his belongings" here on earth. So it is vital to work in close association with this "slave" class and respond in a positive way to the counsel that you receive through it. This is in harmony with what is stated at Revelation 7:9-17. There it is made clear that, in addition to the 144,000 spiritual Israelites who would be "slaves of our God," a "great crowd" of others would stand approved before God and Christ. Their respect for Jehovah's organizational arrangement is made clear, because it is pointed out that they serve God "in his temple," that is, in association on earth with the remnant of Christ's body members, who make up a temple of "living stones," "a holy temple for Jehovah . . . a place for God to inhabit by spirit." (1 Pet. 2:5; Eph. 2:21, 22) And in his illustration of the sheep and the goats, Jesus says that people of the nations are to undergo judicial examination on the basis of their treatment of his "brothers," his spirit-anointed fellow heirs of the heavenly kingdom. It is those who loyally uphold them even when they are being persecuted and who refresh them by wholehearted participation with them as dedicated Christians in God's service who will be approved by Jesus Christ and rewarded with eternal life. —Matt. 25:31-46; Heb. 2:10, 11.

From among the members of Christ's spirit-anointed body members certain ones serve as a visible governing body. In the first century of our Common Era that governing body was made up of the apostles and certain other mature brothers in the Jerusalem congregation. (Acts 15:2, 6, 23) When they were called on to make decisions affecting the lives and activity of God's people, they considered carefully what the Scriptures said about the matter, looked to God for the direction of his spirit, and then gave appropriate counsel. Response to their oversight strengthened the faith of the congregations and resulted in continued increase, with God's blessing.—Acts 16:4, 5; 1 Cor. 3:6, 7.

In order to carry out the preaching work most effectively under modern-day conditions, the "faithful and discreet slave" has organized a legal corporation, the Watch Tower Bible and Tract

Society of Pennsylvania. This Society, made up of mature Christians, is nonprofit and is completely devoted to advancing the interests of true worship in the earth. It has been used by the anointed followers of Jesus Christ for many years in dispensing knowledge to the household of faith and directing the preaching work, and Jehovah's blessing on that arrangement is very manifest. The visible governing body is closely identified with the board of directors of this Society. As was true among early Christians, response to the oversight of the governing body results in unity and increase.

To facilitate the carrying out of Jesus' instructions to preach "this good news of the kingdom" in all the inhabited earth, the Watch Tower Bible and Tract Society also has branch offices in various countries. All of these are subject to the visible governing body, but each branch devotes its attention to its own territory. Knowing the conditions that exist there, the branch office is in position to apply instructions in the most beneficial way and to handle local matters promptly.

It is no less true in our day than it was in the first century of our Common Era that close contact with Jehovah's visible organization is important. Those who got baptized as Christians at the time of Pentecost, 33 C.E., continued in close association with the apostles to receive instruction. (Acts 2:41, 42) When persecution resulted in a scattering of the disciples, they still kept in touch with the governing body in Jerusalem. (Acts 8:1, 14-17) Later, when Saul of Tarsus was converted, the Lord saw to it that he was brought into contact with representatives of the Christian congregation for instruction. (Acts 9:1-22) And as this zealous apostle went about the preaching work, he built up the appreciation of others for Jehovah's visible organization. How? By referring the important circumcision issue to the governing body at Jerusalem and supporting the decision made; also by organizing congregations in many of the cities where he preached. (Acts 14:21-23; 15:1, 2; 16:4, 5) The instructions written to some of those congregations have been preserved for us in the inspired Word of God, and they continue to provide the basis for the organizational procedures followed by Jehovah's Christian witnesses today.

CHAPTER 3

Congregation Meetings

IN ALL parts of the earth where there are groups of Jehovah's witnesses, the Watch Tower Bible and Tract Society has organized congregations and provided a schedule of meetings for the spiritual upbuilding of those associated with them.

Gathering together to hear God's Word and to share in worship is important for each one of us, even as it was in the days of faithful Nehemiah, who urged his fellow Israelites: "We should not neglect the house of our God." (Neh. 10:39) Attending meetings of Jehovah's witnesses shows that you are conscious of your spiritual need and it identifies you with Jehovah's servants in the earth. At Hebrews 10:24, 25, the apostle Paul urges us to appreciate the importance of the meetings, saying: "Let us consider one another to incite to love and fine works, not forsaking the gathering of ourselves together, as some have the custom, but encouraging one another, and all the more so as you behold the day drawing near." That "day" is indeed drawing very near, and the pressures of the world are constantly increasing. So, more than ever before, it is necessary to gather together at the congregation meetings, in order to stay spiritually awake. Even when you are tired at the end of the day, you will find that the meetings are refreshing.

Attending meetings is important for both young persons and those of older years. It is a fine thing when parents arrange to bring their children with them to the meetings. As the prophet Moses instructed the people in his day: "Congregate the people, the men and the women and the little ones . . . in order that they may listen and in order that they may learn." (Deut. 31:12) And of the young man Timothy, the Bible informs us that he knew the holy writings from the time of infancy.—2 Tim. 3:14, 15.

It is not just occasional meeting attendance that makes one a spiritually sound, mature Christian. More is required than that. Regularity is needed, and balance, enabling one to benefit from all the provisions made by Jehovah through his organization. Those who embraced the truth at the time of Pentecost, 33 C.E., did not treat the matter lightly. "They continued devoting themselves to the teaching of the apostles . . . And day after day they were in constant attendance at the temple with one accord." (Acts 2:42, 46) Later, when Paul instructed disciples in Ephesus, he provided a consistent program of spiritual upbuilding for them, giving talks daily. (Acts 19:9) Really, where would we rather be than in association with Jehovah's people? And what could be more beneficial than hearing the Word of God discussed?

It is also our privilege and duty when attending meetings to consider the others who are present. Of course, our being in attendance is itself a source of encouragement to them. But, when discussing the importance of attending meetings, the apostle Paul urged us to do more than simply be present. He said: "Let us hold fast the public declaration of our hope without wavering." (Heb. 10:23) So, when there is opportunity for audience participation, offer to express yourself on the material under consideration. This will deepen the impression on your own mind, strengthen your faith in the matter being discussed and upbuild others who are present. It will also provide a good example for any newly interested ones who are at the meeting with you. Do not feel that what you might say is not of sufficient importance. Your very willingness to comment will warm the hearts of others in attendance, and your accepting the privilege of participating in the meeting will result in rich blessings for you.

Another way that you can be a blessing to others is by inviting and bringing them with you to the meetings of Jehovah's witnesses. Tell your friends and neighbors about the good things that you are learning at the meetings, and invite them to come with you. Freely advertise the meetings both by word of mouth and by distributing handbills when you participate in the field ministry. Right from the start, build up a desire on the part of those with whom you study the Bible to attend meetings. Even in the congregation there may well be some who need encouragement and assistance to get to the meetings. There will be mutual benefit if you are able to extend personal aid to them.

Each one of the meetings is important; each plays a part in your life as a Christian. As we consider the various meetings of the congregation, take note of how that is true.

"WATCHTOWER" STUDY

The weekly study of the *Watchtower* magazine is the most important meeting of the congregation, and everyone associated with the congregation should make a diligent effort to be present regularly. The study material frequently deals with the application of Bible principles to your daily living and fortifies you against the "spirit of the world" and unchristian conduct. (1 Cor. 2:12) Through the columns of *The Watchtower* comes increased light on Bible doctrine and the fulfillment of prophecy as Jehovah makes this known. Regularly sharing in the *Watchtower* study will enable you to keep in sharp focus Jehovah's righteous new system of things. It will assist you to manifest the fruitage of God's spirit in your life and keep strong your desire to serve Jehovah zealously. (Gal. 5:22, 23) It will fortify you for the searching trials of faith that lie ahead for each one of us. It will help you to prove worthy of perfect life in God's promised new order under his everlasting kingdom of righteousness.

The schedule for study of the principal articles in each issue of *The Watchtower* is printed right in the magazine, so each one can know in advance what material will be discussed. You will find it very beneficial to set aside time during the week to read the lesson and look up the scriptures before you attend the meeting. This will enable you to participate, and you will also find that you get far more from the expressions made by others.

Even if you should find that, on occasion, you are not able to study your lesson in advance, do not miss the meeting. By being present you will benefit from the preparation that others have done. Their comments will help you to understand matters that may not have been clear to you, and even hearing them express themselves on truths with which you are well acquainted will deepen your appreciation; it will help to fortify your heart. (Prov. 4:4, 23) Furthermore, the *Watchtower* study servant will endeavor to handle the meeting in such a way that principal points are emphasized for the benefit of everyone. Even more important, keep in mind what Jesus Christ said: "Where there are two or three gathered

together in my name, there I am in their midst."
—Matt. 18:20.

The *Watchtower* study is opened and closed
with song and prayer. After the opening prayer
the conductor briefly draws attention to a few
high points in the lesson, both to whet the audience's appetite for what is to follow and to help
them to appreciate the reason for considering
the specific material at hand. If it is a continua-
tion of an article started the previous week, he
may briefly restate certain key points from that
earlier study and tie them in with what is next
to be considered. The printed questions provided
in *The Watchtower* are propounded, then the study
conductor calls on those who volunteer by raising
their hands. Feel free to express yourself. He
usually directs attention to the scriptures in the
paragraph, encouraging comments that show their
relation to the question being considered. If time
allows, he also calls for the reading of certain
scriptures that are cited but not quoted. Then
the paragraph is read in summary. For reading
the paragraphs a different reader may be used
each week, and, if possible, advance selection is
made of a well-qualified reader, since much valuable instruction is imparted when the reading
is done with proper sense stress and enthusiasm.
If there is only one brother capable of doing good
reading, then he may be asked to read every week.
If you are a brother who can read effectively, or
if you apply yourself and become a fine public
reader, it may be your privilege to serve the congregation in this way on occasion.

Ordinarily, the *Watchtower* study is just one
hour in length, with no more than ten additional
minutes for the opening and closing, including
announcements. You can help to keep the study
within the allotted time by having comments ready
to offer as soon as the questions are asked. This
will keep the study moving and make it possible

for the congregation to hear from many persons during the time set aside for the study.

In most cases the entire congregation gathers together at the Kingdom Hall for their weekly *Watchtower* study. However, if some live at distant points, far from the Kingdom Hall, *Watchtower* studies are sometimes arranged for them, perhaps on Sundays or another day that is convenient for them. It is better to have a *Watchtower* study in their own locality than for them to miss it because of the long distance and inconvenience in traveling to the central meeting. In such cases a brother living in that vicinity is appointed as the study conductor.

The meeting is held in the language of the country or district, unless the congregation was specifically organized to serve a different language group. However, if there is a group of persons in the congregation who speak another tongue, there is no objection to arranging a *Watchtower* study for the benefit of these brothers. They will get a clearer understanding by studying *The Watchtower* in their own language and expressing themselves in their own tongue. The extra-language meetings should be at a time different from the regular meetings for the congregation, however, and those attending these meetings should also be encouraged to attend the regular meetings of the congregation, to get acquainted with the language of the land where they dwell. In this way they will, in time, be able to have a more extensive share in the ministry.

THE PUBLIC MEETING

The public meeting is quite different from the *Watchtower* study. Rather than being a question-and-answer discussion of printed study material, it generally takes the form of a discourse. But to stimulate keen interest and to impress key thoughts on the minds of everyone, the speaker may use pictures, maps or an outline of points on a blackboard. As part of the program, arrangements may be made for questions both to and from the audience. At times, the material may be presented by a symposium of speakers.

A wide variety of subjects comes under consideration at this meeting. There are talks about marital problems and the difficult situations that confront youths in this modern world. Christian morals are discussed. The marvels of creation and scientific confirmation of the Scriptures are considered. Other talks provide illuminating background information to enhance your appreciation of Bible accounts, as well as comments on their significance in our day. There are verse-by-verse commentaries on portions of the Bible. Films produced by the Society may also be presented from time to time as part of the public meeting program. In addition, other topics that are particularly appropriate to your community or needed by your congregation may be developed and presented locally. Truly, the public meeting provides a spiritual feast.

This is called a *public* meeting because extensive advertising is done to invite the public and the talks are given with the public in mind. Not that the material is directed solely to the public, but the speaker makes it a point to explain his subject in terms that the public can grasp. He frequently invites his audience to open the Bible and follow with him as he reads from it, just as you might do in personal discussion with a newly interested person in his home. Anyone who attends cannot help but be impressed with the fact that here are a people who truly do study and believe God's Word. As a result, sincere ones will be moved to declare: "God is really among you."—1 Cor. 14:25.

Since this is advertised as a public meeting, and the public are invited simply to hear a Bible discussion, we do not open and close this meeting with prayer, thus obliging them to join in worship with us. Rather, a chairman usually makes a few opening remarks, welcoming those present, introducing the speaker and stating the title of the talk for the day. His remarks are very brief. After the talk, the chairman also concludes the meeting, making whatever announcements are appropriate for those present. In most cases he will let you know the title of the next public talk and the name of the speaker. He will also warmly invite everyone to remain for the *Watchtower* study, if it is held after the public talk. When there are new ones on hand, he may extend an invitation for them to avail themselves of our free home Bible study service; and perhaps a tract or a booklet and a handbill listing the congregation's meetings will be given to them before they leave.

You have a key role to play in connection with this meeting. Of course, your presence is necessary if the meeting is going to accomplish for the members of the congregation what is intended. But there is something more than that. The congregation counts on you to advertise the talk, both by distributing handbills (sometimes by using placards) and by enthusiastically talking to your acquaintances and other interested persons, stimulating their desire to be present. Where possible, arrange for others to come to the meeting right along with you. This is by far the most effective means of building up attendance.

If there are sufficient qualified speakers available, your congregation will no doubt have a public talk every week. Frequently this can be made possible by arranging for visiting speakers from nearby congregations. But, even if there is a shortage of speakers in your area, arrangements will be made to have these talks just as often as possible, so that the congregation does not miss

out on the fine instruction made available by
means of them.

In addition to putting on talks in your Kingdom
Hall, arrangements may be made for holding
public talks in rural sections and outlying towns
in the congregation's territory. Efforts are made
to give a thorough witness in this territory in
conjunction with the public meetings. If there
are many locations that can be obtained, such
as community houses, lodge halls, schools, private
homes of Kingdom publishers, lawns, fields and
parks, the congregation will no doubt plan on
using some of them. Usually they can be obtained
at a very reasonable cost or even free. If you have
a share in setting up sound equipment for such
a meeting, keep in mind that you should conform
to local regulations as to operating the equipment.
The loudspeakers need only be loud enough to
reach the audience so that all can hear well.

Public meetings similar to those enjoyed by
each congregation of Jehovah's witnesses were
also conducted by Jesus Christ, his apostles and
their associates. Often they spoke in synagogues,
which were actually public assembly halls in those
days. (John 18:20; Acts 17:1-3) Paul used a
school auditorium in Ephesus as a place to give
talks. (Acts 19:8, 9) Other discourses were given
on the mountainside and down by the sea. (Matt.
5:1, 2; 13:1, 2) Not only the public, but the disciples were very much encouraged by the things
that they learned from these discourses. (Matt.
7:28; Luke 6:17, 20) That will be your experience
too as you regularly attend the public meetings.

THE SERVICE MEETING

The service meeting is specifically designed to
equip you to have an effective share in carrying
out the work of preaching the Kingdom good news
and making disciples of those who respond to
God's Word. (Matt. 24:14) Featured at this meet-

ing are talks that highlight the Scriptural methods to use in the field ministry, and encouraging experiences are related in connection with the preaching work, both locally and in other parts of the world. There are demonstrations designed to show effective ways to introduce the Kingdom message to people and stimulate their interest in God's Word, also how to cope with the various obstacles and objections common to the territory in which you live. Practical instruction is given on the way to conduct home Bible studies and aid interested ones to begin to associate with the congregation. The meeting aids both new and seasoned Witnesses to improve their ability in the service of God. Regularity in attending the service meeting results in unified activity on the part of the entire congregation and it will aid you to be regular in the field service. Since every baptized witness of Jehovah is a minister, this meeting is important for all of us and it is also very beneficial for anyone else who desires to become a dedicated servant of God. Make attendance at this meeting a part of your weekly schedule of activity.

Meetings of this sort are nothing new. They are based on sound Scriptural precedent. Before sending his disciples out to preach, Jesus gave them detailed instructions on what to say and do. (Matt. 10:5–11:1; Luke 10:1-16) Later his disciples continued to have such meetings at which they discussed their experiences in the field ministry and were strengthened for continued service. (Acts 4:23-31) We continue the practice today.

Service meetings are built around the information provided by the Society in *Kingdom Ministry,* which you will receive every month from your congregation overseer. When he receives a new issue of *Kingdom Ministry,* he carefully analyzes what it contains and assigns the various meeting parts to qualified brothers, giving them written notice of their assignments as soon as possible. But there is more to it, in order to make the meetings most practical and beneficial to the local congregation. He may review the counsel given by the circuit servant on his latest report and see that this is taken into consideration at various times during the month. He also endeavors to discuss with each one on the program how to present his material in a way that will most directly fit the local needs. At times he may even rearrange the program in order to take up some matter that is urgently in need of attention. Arrangements should also be made to rehearse demonstrations and to coordinate all the meeting parts. This takes time, but it results in a program that is informative and spiritually upbuilding.

From time to time there is a service meeting that is left for the overseer of the local congregation to outline. Others of the servants may also have some suggestions, and he will take these into consideration. Since the overseer is well acquainted with the needs of the congregation, he can see that the meeting is one that contains practical suggestions that will be of real benefit to the publishers.

Every service meeting is opened with song and prayer and closes in the same manner, unless one meeting follows the other. There is also a discussion of the day's text. At the close of the program service arrangements are outlined for the days ahead, also there frequently is some announcement about what has been planned for forthcoming meetings.

At almost every service meeting there is opportunity for you to participate. Avail yourself of it. If there is to be a question-and-answer discussion of material from *Kingdom Ministry* or some other publication, endeavor to read it ahead of time so that you will be in position to comment.

Or if you are invited to relate a field experience or to share in a demonstration, gladly accept this privilege, if at all possible, and work at it diligently. Attend the service meeting with the thought of giving, not merely receiving.

Dedicated and baptized males who have the needed ability and who set a good example as Christians are put in charge of the various service meeting parts. If you are a brother, and you apply yourself diligently, it may be your privilege to serve the congregation in this way. Accept such assignments joyfully, and care for them conscientiously as part of your service to Jehovah. When you are assigned such a meeting part, study carefully the material provided by the Society. Determine what the principal points of instruction are and emphasize them so that the publishers will understand and remember them. There are many ways in which material can be effectively presented. Demonstrations, round-table discussions, interviews, quizzes, forums, dialogues, question-and-answer sessions and service talks may all be used at various times. Have in mind, too, the importance of applying the material to the situation of the local congregation. If you are not sure what is needed in this regard, discuss the matter with your congregation overseer. An ideal presentation is one that is simple, practical and to the point.

Demonstrations may be called for at times. Any publishers in good standing with the congregation, including young children, may be used in these presentations. In fact, it is a good thing, from time to time, to afford opportunity for every publisher in the congregation to have a share in these programs. If you are assigned to present a demonstration, do not try to put over some great dramatic production with a lot of stage props. Use natural scenes, such as a house-to-house visit, a back-call, a home Bible study or a family discussion. It is what is said and how it is said that are important, not the stage setting. To be effective, demonstrations must be well rehearsed. Do this either in someone's home or at the Kingdom Hall itself, so that each one will know where he is to be and what he is to say and do. In that way the demonstration will proceed smoothly and will accomplish its purpose.

Each service meeting has a theme. The first meeting in the month is built around the service theme shown on the Society's calendar and in the *Yearbook*. Other meetings may be built around other appropriate themes. The meeting will make a more lasting impression on the minds of the publishers if each one will tie in his part with the theme; so take this into consideration when preparing your assigned part. Also, consider the timing. If each one on the program sticks to the allotted time, the meeting will conclude in one hour, apart from the song and prayer. Everyone who shares in the program should cooperate to that end.

THEOCRATIC MINISTRY SCHOOL

In addition to the other meetings, each congregation of Jehovah's witnesses provides a Theocratic Ministry School. This is a continuous training school for men, women and children. There are special textbooks and a well-planned program of activity. As a part of this course, periodically those in attendance read the entire Bible, analyze the principles of effective speaking and discuss how to conduct effective congregation meetings. Students also give short talks to the group and practice sermons to individuals, and a qualified counselor offers helpful suggestions for improvement.

In organizing and conducting this meeting, Jehovah's witnesses show that they take to heart the practical counsel that the apostle Paul gave to Timothy, a fellow servant of the Lord, when he said: "Continue applying yourself to public reading, to exhortation, to teaching. . . . Ponder over these things; be absorbed in them, that your advancement may be manifest to all persons." (1 Tim. 4:13-15) By enrolling in the Theocratic Ministry School, which convenes once each week at the Kingdom Hall, you show that you, too, are interested in advancement. Such training can aid you to become a more effective public praiser of Jehovah. It can equip you to accomplish more in the time you have available for the field ministry, as well as to give fine comments in the congregation meetings. In the case of brothers, this training is one of the important steps toward qualifying for the privilege of taking responsibility for service meeting parts and delivering public talks, and it is a means by which you can develop the abilities required of those who are appointed as overseers of Jehovah's people.

All persons associated with the congregation, both male and female, are encouraged to enroll in the Theocratic Ministry School and attend regularly. Those enrolled will be assigned periodically to give student talks, and they will be notified well in advance so that they can prepare thoroughly. Though no roll call is read at the school, it is beneficial to be present, and it is particularly important to be on hand to give any talks that are assigned to you. Plan to get to the hall before the meeting starts, so the school servant will know that you are going to give the talk. If an emergency situation arises, and it is impossible to be present to fulfill an assignment, be sure to notify the school servant, doing so just as early as possible so that he can arrange for someone else to prepare the talk.

When you are assigned to give a talk in the Theocratic Ministry School, keep in mind that the reason for your giving the talk is twofold: It provides opportunity for you to improve your speaking ability, and at the same time you cover instructive material for the benefit of everyone present. To accomplish these objectives, it is important to spend some time analyzing the speech qualities on which you are assigned to work, as well as to study the information that will be discussed in your talk. If you do this, each talk you give will reflect improvement in your speaking ability.

After each student talk the instructor will offer helpful counsel. So, if you will be giving a talk, before the meeting be sure to give him your Speech Counsel slip, because he will want to make notations on it. If you have done well on certain speech qualities, he will commend you, and, to the extent that time permits, he may point out, for the benefit of everyone present, what it was that made them good and how they affect our ministry. If further work on a speech quality would be advantageous, he will offer suggestions to assist you. Always keep in mind that the counsel given is for your edification and to assist you to be a better praiser of Jehovah God.

In addition to the student talks, the school program usually includes an instruction talk, given by the school servant or one of the better qualified brothers enrolled in the school. If you apply yourself diligently (and are a male), in time it may be your privilege to give such discourses. There is also provision on most weeks for an oral review of the previous week's instruction talk, and it will be stimulating to you, and beneficial to the others too, if you prepare ahead of time and volunteer to answer at least one of those review questions. Then, too, periodically there may be a written review of the information that has been studied. This is not for competitive purposes but is a means of helping you to see if you have an accurate understanding of the material that has been discussed, and it assists you to learn any key points that you may have missed. Avail yourself of all these opportunities to be an active participant in the Theocratic Ministry School. Even those who are unable to give talks, because of some infirmity or because they are too young, should attend and benefit from the instruction provided.

CONGREGATION BOOK STUDY

The congregation book study is generally conducted with a smaller group than the other meetings. There are just a few families or a comparatively small number of individuals who gather at each of these studies. Instead of having the entire congregation come together at one place for the meeting, arrangements are made for them to meet in convenient locations scattered throughout the congregation's territory. One group may meet at the Kingdom Hall; others assemble in the homes of persons who have kindly opened them for that purpose. Here is an evidence of Jehovah's loving-kindness and his tender care for his people, because in these small groups it is possible for more personal attention to be given to the spiritual growth of each individual.—Isa. 40:11.

This is a one-hour group study, using the Bible and a textbook provided by the Watch Tower Bible and Tract Society. Here a careful study is made of Bible doctrines, prophecy, counsel on Christian conduct and other information that will aid you to carry out your dedication to Jehovah God. Scriptures cited in the study material are looked up in the Bible and their relation to the points under discussion is analyzed. Time is taken to discuss the material thoroughly. As you attend this study week by week, you will find that you gain not only knowledge but understanding; you will learn the reasons for statements that are made and how to support them from the Bible.

(Prov. 4:1; 2 Tim. 2:15) You will learn how to conduct discussions of the same material with individuals and families that you are able to help to become acquainted with the "word of life." (Phil. 2:16) This meeting will do much to equip you to become a capable teacher of God's Word.

Basically, the meeting is conducted in the same manner as the *Watchtower* study. It is opened and closed with prayer. Questions are asked on each paragraph; comments are invited; scriptures are read; then the paragraph is read in summary. However, at the congregation book study there is no set amount of material to be covered, so more time can be spent in discussing the material. The important thing is not how many pages are covered but that those present understand what has been studied. To impress principal thoughts on the mind of each one, brief oral reviews are generally conducted at both the beginning and the end of the study.

With a small group such as this, there is more opportunity for you to comment. You will find that it is not at all difficult to participate freely at this meeting, and this gives you opportunity to get accustomed to making a declaration of your faith before others. (Heb. 13:15) It is good to learn to make your comments in your own words, instead of reading them out of the book, because this enables you to determine whether you really understand the material. Learn to give simple, clear, brief comments, because they are the easiest to follow and, therefore, the best for you to use in teaching others. To get the most out of the study, set aside time to prepare your lesson in advance.

Although everyone present is encouraged to share in the reading of scriptures, just one person reads the paragraphs each week. If possible, arrangements are made for a well-qualified dedicated brother to be the reader. If there is not one available, other than the conductor himself, he may ask a dedicated sister or, in some cases, an undedicated person to do the reading. Assignment to read the paragraphs is usually made a week in advance. If that should be your privilege, be sure to prepare well, realizing that effective reading adds much to the instructive value of the meeting.

Having these study groups scattered throughout the congregation territory makes it convenient both for you and for newly interested persons in the neighborhood to attend. Make every effort to bring others with you to the meeting, so that they can get a taste of the spiritually upbuilding discussions and warm association that we enjoy. From time to time as you call on these people, why not take along various ones from your congregation book study group? When the interested person gets acquainted with a number of those who attend the study, it will make it easier for him to respond to your invitation to come.

In addition to providing a study place, the location where the congregation book study is held is also a rendezvous for service. Here the group can meet at convenient times to go out into the field ministry.

When your congregation book study group grows to the point that there are about twenty in regular attendance, then the congregation overseer will consider arranging for another study group. Of course, this means that another mature study conductor will also be needed, and, if you meet the Scriptural requirements, that may be your privilege. (1 Tim. 3:8-10, 12, 13) Also, another home will be needed where the new group can meet. It should be one that is neat and clean, and located where it will be convenient for a group of publishers to meet so that none will have to travel very far. It is truly a privilege for one's home to serve as a place for worship in the community, and such an arrangement often results in rich spiritual blessings to the members of the household. If you would like to have a congregation book study in your home, why not mention it to your overseer? Then, when the need arises, he will know that there is a location available. Having congregation meetings in private homes was a practice of the early Christians, and the practice has continued to have Jehovah's blessing in our day.—Rom. 16:3, 5; Philem. 1, 2.

TIME OF MEETINGS

The times at which the congregation meetings are held are determined locally. They may vary from place to place, because the matter is discussed with the congregation and then times are chosen that are convenient for the majority of publishers in the congregation.

The greater number of congregations have their public meeting and *Watchtower* study on Sunday. Then, one night early in the week they have their congregation book study, and another night later in the week they have their Theocratic Ministry School and service meeting. But this varies. If some have to travel for many hours to get to the meetings, or other circumstances make it necessary, they may have more of their meetings at one time.

In areas where most of the brothers work late, the schedule may be adjusted to fit their situation. There are some congregations that do not start their week-night meetings until quite late; others have meetings in the afternoon. Of course, in locations where more than one congregation uses the same Kingdom Hall, meeting times have to be set accordingly.

A large number of publishers engage in the field ministry on Sunday. Many of them prefer to do their field service early in the day, and then gather for congregation meetings in the afternoon or at night. But some have found that, because of the way of life in their locality, they get a more favorable response in the field ministry on Sunday afternoon than in the morning; so they have their meetings in the morning. Either is all right.

KINGDOM HALL

The Kingdom Hall of Jehovah's Witnesses is the center of pure worship in the community. It is the principal location where meetings of the congregation are held, and it provides a central place from which the field ministry can be conducted.

In some communities a congregation may be small and so may meet in a private home. But just as soon as it proves to be both possible and practical, each congregation endeavors to obtain an adequate meeting hall. In some localities it is more convenient to rent a hall than to buy or to build. However, large numbers of congregations have decided to purchase property and build their own Kingdom Hall, suited to their needs. It is up to each congregation to decide what it wants to do in this matter. Kingdom Halls are ordinarily moderate in size. Emphasis is placed on the spiritual condition of the congregation rather than the size of the building. Of course, whether you own or rent your hall, it ought to be kept clean, and that is a responsibility that each one in the congregation should help to bear. Both inside and out, the Kingdom Hall should be a proper representation of Jehovah's organization. Usually the congregation overseer works out a schedule for the various congregation book study groups to take turns in cleaning the hall, along with a list of the things that need to be done each week. When your study group's turn comes, be sure to do your part.

There are a number of things that can be done to advertise the Kingdom Hall. For one thing, there should be a sign out in front bearing the words "Kingdom Hall of Jehovah's Witnesses" and an up-to-date listing of the times of meetings. If your hall has a window on street level, it is good to have an attractive display of literature so that passersby may observe it. Perhaps you enjoy arranging things in an artistic manner; if so, you may want to volunteer to help keep that display up-to-date and clean, using current literature and changing the arrangement from time to time. Some newspapers gladly publish free notices of meeting times and special events, and it is good to take advantage of this service. It may also be that the congregation servant will want to have his phone listed under "Jehovah's Witnesses."

Besides the above means of advertising, do not fail to make good use of any handbills provided by your congregation. Distribute them freely. They provide an excellent reminder to the people in your territory that Jehovah's witnesses are active among them and are ready and willing to help them.

Of course, it costs money to keep up a Kingdom Hall, and all those associated with the congregation have the privilege of contributing financially to its maintenance. There is never any solicitation of funds, nor is a collection ever taken up. But a contribution box is provided in the Kingdom Hall so that each one can contribute as he is able, 'not under compulsion' but "just as he has resolved in his heart."—2 Cor. 9:7; 8:12.

At every meeting in the Kingdom Hall there should be a brother who serves as an attendant, and he ought to be a person who has a friendly personality. Would you be willing to serve in this capacity occasionally? Speak to your overseer about it. Then, if you are assigned, keep in mind that it is your job to greet newcomers and to make them feel welcome. Also, be sure that there are sufficient chairs set up and that any necessary attention is given to proper heating and ventilation in the hall.

In addition to its use for regular congregation meetings and as a rendezvous for field service, the Kingdom Hall may be used for wedding ceremonies and funeral services, with the permission of the congregation service committee. It is up to the committee to decide what preparations for such events may be made in the hall and what announcements of such use of the hall will be made to the congregation, if the individuals concerned would like to have the congregation know. When the need arises, the congregation will furnish a speaker for a funeral service, whether it is conducted in the Kingdom Hall or elsewhere; or, if a particular person is requested, and he is able to handle it, that is all right. If requested, the overseer will also be glad to arrange for a capable brother to conduct a wedding ceremony, in harmony with the local legal requirements.

CIRCUIT AND DISTRICT ASSEMBLIES

Everyone who regularly attends the meetings at the Kingdom Hall also looks forward with eager anticipation to the larger assemblies of Jehovah's people that are held periodically. The coming together of large numbers of Jehovah's people for instruction has long been a feature of true worship. (Neh. 8:1-3; Deut. 16:1-16; 31:10-13) Such assemblies are highlights in the lives of Jehovah's witnesses today.

Twice a year a number of congregations that are served by the same circuit servant meet together for a three-day circuit assembly. There are talks and demonstrations, practical instruction designed to meet the needs of that circuit. Such assemblies also afford opportunity for those who have recently made a dedication to Jehovah God to symbolize it by water immersion. Additionally, once a year a number of circuits usually gather for what is called a district assembly. At these district assemblies, and at the occasional national and international assemblies, some of the most thrilling discourses and announcements in the modern-day history of Jehovah's people have been presented. It is not only the last day or two of such assemblies that are important; right from the opening session on, the program contains material that has been specially prepared to equip you to be a more effective praiser of Jehovah and to endure faithfully in his service right on into his new system of things. If at all possible, plan ahead so that you can enjoy the entire assembly.

The very fact that a large number of persons who manifest the spirit of God have come together makes people ask questions, as they did at Pentecost in the year 33 C.E. As a result, conventions of Jehovah's people afford an opportunity to give a witness to God's kingdom in an impressive way. (Acts 2:1-42) The love that motivates Jehovah's witnesses to contribute their time and labor to serve their Christian brothers by operating the various assembly departments is a source of amazement to the world, resulting in an effective witness.—John 13:34, 35.

Not only must those in attendance have their spiritual needs cared for through the program itself, but also their physical needs require attention. Sufficient rooming accommodations must be obtained. Usually the hotels do not have enough rooms for our large conventions; besides, many of the delegates who come as family groups are of moderate means, and they need something economical. This calls for house-to-house visits to contact local residents who are willing to rent rooms at reasonable rates. Food is made available through the Cafeteria and Refreshment departments at the assembly and is served to conventioners for a moderate price. Attendants are also required. These and many other services necessary to the operation of the assembly are performed by volunteer workers attending the assembly. None of them are paid for their work, but they willingly serve out of love for their Christian brothers. (Ps. 110:3) When you attend assemblies, it is your privilege to volunteer to share in this helpful service. If you are able to do so, you will find that your enjoyment of the assembly itself will be greatly increased, because, as the Lord Jesus said, "there is more happiness in giving than there is in receiving."—Acts 20:35.

PERSONAL AND FAMILY STUDY

Having individually dedicated ourselves to Jehovah, we show that we take delight in him and the things he says. We do not feel that it is a burden to study and discuss the Scriptures. These things fill our hearts and minds and, as a result, we seek out opportunities to read the Bible and our Bible-study aids. We are like that person of whom the psalm says: "His delight is in the law of Jehovah, and in his law he reads in an undertone day and night." (Ps. 1:2) With all our heart we join with the writer of the 119th Psalm, who said to God: "How I do love your law! All day long it is my concern. How smooth to my palate your sayings have been, more so than honey to my mouth! Your word is a lamp to my foot, and a light to my roadway." (Ps. 119:97, 103, 105) Feeling this way about it, we do not limit our consideration of God's Word to the time that we are at the Kingdom Hall. Rather, we endeavor to make some time for it every day in our own homes.

If your family is united in the pure worship of Jehovah, you will want to do some of your studying as a family group. The Bible particularly urges parents to feel the responsibility that is theirs to inculcate godly thinking in their off-

spring. (Eph. 6:4; Deut. 6:1, 6, 7; Ps. 78:3, 4)
What a blessing to the household when this is
done! The family is drawn closer together, and the
fruitage of God's spirit manifest in their lives
makes the home a truly happy one. The children
get their feet firmly planted on the way that leads
to everlasting life. (Prov. 22:6) So, when you
sit down to a meal together, you will want to
follow the Christian practice of giving thanks
to God before you eat. (Matt. 14:19; Acts 27:35;
Luke 11:2, 3) And at a meal when you are all
together you will find it most beneficial to take
some time to read and discuss the Scripture text
and comments for the day provided in the *Yearbook of Jehovah's Witnesses*, if it is available in
your language. If you do not have the *Yearbook*
in your tongue, you will find the texts published
in *The Watchtower*. Endeavor to bring each member of the family into the discussion. Many families also enjoy reading at this time some of the
experiences found in the *Yearbook*. Such a practice
can make mealtime in your home a most pleasant
and spiritually upbuilding occasion.—Rom. 14:19.

Apart from your regular discussion of the day's
text, it is a good thing to have an evening, or
other convenient time, set aside for family Bible
study. There are many publications available for
you to study together. You may want to prepare
together for one of the congregation meetings,
or you may choose to study something else. Select
the material that is most appropriate to the needs
of your household. The time to be devoted to such
a study on any one occasion and the amount of
material covered can best be worked out in each
family. Take time to look up scriptures together.
Discuss points thoroughly so that everyone understands them. Emphasize their value in your everyday lives. If you do, this time spent together each
week will be a major contribution to the spiritual
growth of your family.

Of course, it is unlikely that you will do all your reading and studying together. There is also a need to do some on a personal basis, and it has been found that the rate of one's spiritual development usually bears a direct relationship to his personal study habits. Jehovah God counseled Joshua in ancient times that he needed regular personal study of the Scriptures to succeed as a servant of God. (Josh. 1:8) The same is true of us today.

Some of your personal study will no doubt be preparation for congregation meetings; some will be reading of the Bible and other publications. Lovingly, the "faithful and discreet slave" has provided an abundance of fine material to use. In addition to bound books and booklets, there is *The Watchtower,* which is the principal magazine of Jehovah's witnesses. *Awake!,* also published in many languages, reports on world news and helps one to get a theocratic perspective on a wide variety of topics. To the extent that you are able to read these publications as they are made available, there is a blessing in store for you. Of course, some have more time to read than others; some read faster than others; some can grasp things more quickly than can others. But the Society has supplied ample for everyone. By availing yourself of it, to the extent that your personal circumstances permit, you will be protected against the spirit of the world, strengthened in faith and equipped to be a better servant of Jehovah God. —Phil. 4:8; Rom. 12:2.

CHAPTER 4
Your Field Ministry

NINETEEN hundred years ago when the Lord Jesus Christ was a man on earth he provided for us a pattern of the worship that Jehovah God approves. More than once while His Son was on earth, Jehovah spoke out from the heavens in approval of him. Not only did He do this at the time of Jesus' baptism, but toward the conclusion of Jesus' earthly ministry God again declared, in the hearing of a group of Jesus' disciples: "This is my Son, the beloved, whom I have approved; listen to him." (Matt. 17:5; 3:17) So it is with keen interest that we take note of what Jesus himself did in Jehovah's service and what he instructed his followers to do.

Some months after his immersion in water by John the Baptist, Jesus entered the synagogue in Nazareth, where he had been reared, and read to those there assembled his commission from God, saying: "Jehovah's spirit is upon me, because he anointed me to declare good news to the poor, he sent me forth to preach a release to the captives and a recovery of sight to the blind, to send the crushed ones away with a release, to preach Jehovah's acceptable year." (Luke 4:16-21; Isa. 61:1, 2) Faithfully he carried out that commission. From city to city and village to village, both in the homes of the people and in public places, he went preaching "the good news of the kingdom of God." (Luke 8:1; Matt. 9:35) As he went he gave his followers instructions on how to perform the same kind of ministry.—Matt. 10:7, 11-13.

Then, after his resurrection, Jesus appeared again to his disciples and said to them: "Go therefore and make disciples of people of all the nations, baptizing them in the name of the Father and of the Son and of the holy spirit, teaching them to observe all the things I have commanded you." (Matt. 28:19, 20) They appreciated the importance of that work and, even when persecuted, they continued "declaring the good news of the word." (Acts 8:4) Later, the apostle Paul was also moved by holy spirit to point out how vital this public proclamation of God's Word is to the preacher himself, saying: "With the heart one exercises faith for righteousness, but with the mouth one makes public declaration for salvation." (Rom. 10:10) And of our own day, Jesus foretold: "This good news of the kingdom will be preached in all the inhabited earth for a witness to all the nations; and then the end will come." (Matt. 24: 14) Obviously, those who would do this preaching would be faithful followers of Jesus Christ. So, if you are a true Christian, that prophetic declaration is your commission as a preacher of the kingdom of God.

If you are a dedicated and baptized Christian, you are an ordained minister of Jehovah God. You did not ordain yourself by vowing to serve God, nor did the one baptizing you ordain you. God's commission to all those dedicating themselves to do His will is what constitutes your ordination as a minister. While God's commandment to preach the Kingdom good news is there in the Bible for all to read, it constitutes the ordination only of those who meet his requirements. It may be compared to the issuing of a diploma to a school graduate. While the wording of the diplomas is basically the same, and anyone can read them, what they say does not apply to everyone. One's name belongs on such a diploma only when he meets the requirements. Likewise, it is after study, dedication and baptism that the commission from God recorded in the Bible constitutes one's ordination. Of course, seminary training and written certificates of ordination are not requirements for Scriptural ordination. (John 7:14, 15; Acts 4:13) Rather, ministers ordained by Jehovah God and backed up by his holy spirit produce living letters of recommendation.—2 Cor. 3:1-3.

Your ministry is not something to treat lightly; it should influence your entire life as a Christian. (1 Cor. 10:31) To care for it requires time, but not merely leftover time or time when you do not happen to have anything else to do. God's Word advises: "Keep strict watch that how you walk is not as unwise but as wise persons, buying out the opportune time for yourselves, because the days are wicked." (Eph. 5:15, 16) That does not mean that you are to take time away from other Christian responsibilities—that you are to neglect study of the Bible or attending congregation meetings, or that you are to fail to perform your Scriptural duties toward your family—and then use this time in the field ministry. Balance should be maintained in caring for all the responsibilities that fall on you as a Christian. In harmony with this, Colossians 4:5 associates our buying out of time with "walking in wisdom toward those on the outside." Yes, time that was formerly used in worldly associations and activities is what ought to be 'bought out' for Christian service. Also, by better organization of personal affairs you may be able to make more time for the ministry. Just how much time you will be able to spend in the ministry is something that you must decide, but do not leave it to chance. Much more will be accomplished, and with better results, if you schedule regular times each week to participate in this most important preaching work.

As was true of Jesus Christ, who set the example for us, when you share in this preaching work you will not speak 'of your own originality.' (John

7:16-18) Where you can find a hearing ear, you will want to reason with the householder from the Scriptures. (Acts 17:2-4) Additionally, the Society has published Bibles and printed sermons in books, booklets and magazines. These may be presented to the people so that, when you are not at the home talking to them, they can read and study on their own, using their own Bible to look up the scriptures cited. In doing this work Jehovah's witnesses are not salesmen or peddlers. They do not seek to make a financial profit from their distribution of literature. It is simply left with interested persons for a small contribution sufficient to cover the cost of printing and handling these publications. Many of the persons met in the witnessing work are unable to contribute, and so millions of copies of booklets, magazines and tracts are given away yearly so that these persons, too, can benefit from the message of salvation that they contain. (2 Cor. 2:17) In their use of such literature, Jehovah's witnesses of today are like their early Christian brothers who, according to historians, were pioneers in the use of the codex, or leaf book, for reproducing the Holy Scriptures.

No doubt, there will be times when you, like many others, feel inadequate for the work of preaching and teaching the Bible. But, remember, it is not one's personal ability that qualifies him to be a minister of God. As the apostle Paul reminded the brothers in Corinth: "Our being adequately qualified issues from God." (2 Cor. 3:4-6) Of far greater importance than any natural ability on your part is your willingness to be used by God. Remember, Moses felt that an impediment of speech disqualified him and Jeremiah said that he was too young, but both of them took up their assignments from God, and how marvelously Jehovah used them! You, too, show yourself to be willing. Regularly attend the meetings that Jehovah has provided to train you. Pray to him for guidance, and you will find great joy in realizing that he is using you and that the power beyond what is normal is from God and not out of yourself.—2 Cor. 4:1, 7.

As you call at the homes of the people, keep in mind the fine counsel that Jesus gave to a group of seventy of his disciples when he sent them out. He said: "Wherever you enter into a house say first, 'May this house have peace.' And if a friend of peace is there, your peace will rest upon him. But if there is not, it will turn back to you." (Luke 10:5, 6) You have a wonderful message, a comforting one, to share with persons who have receptive hearts. Those who are sheeplike will respond to the call of the Fine Shepherd extended through you. (John 10:4, 14-16) Your objective, in harmony with Jesus' prophetic declaration at Matthew 24:14, is to tell others the good news of the Kingdom "for a witness." But we have no reason to expect the whole world to be converted as a result of our preaching.

It is always a happifying experience to find people who listen appreciatively to the Kingdom message, and you will no doubt have many such experiences. (Luke 10:1, 17; Acts 15:3) But the accomplishment of your ministry is not to be measured merely by the number who show interest in the truth of God's Word, nor is it to be measured solely by the amount of literature that you are able to place. Even if those people on whom you call do not accept the good news you bring to them and even if they do not listen to more than a few sentences of what you say, by your very presence at their doors the name of God and the Kingdom message are kept before them. In that way Jehovah's purpose is being accomplished, and you are having a share in it. (Rom. 9:17; Mark 13:10) The very fact that you are regularly participating in the ministry gives evidence of your loving devotion to Jehovah, and this, in turn, makes His heart glad.—1 John 5:3; Prov. 27:11.

Though people show themselves indifferent or unfriendly, do not hold back from giving them further opportunities to hear. Many who at one time turned away the Witnesses who called at their doors are now grateful for the patient perseverance shown by those publishers who called repeatedly and, as a result, they are now our spiritual brothers and sisters with the prospect of everlasting life. Perhaps you yourself are such a person. Oftentimes, people who do not listen believe that their own religion is right, or they may have become embittered by personal experiences in life, or perhaps they have been told lies about us. It is as the apostle Paul wrote at 2 Corinthians 4:4: "The god of this system of things has blinded the minds of the unbelievers, that the illumination of the glorious good news about the Christ, who is the image of God, might not shine through." By kindness on your part, "instructing with mildness those not favorably disposed," you may be able to help them. As Paul wrote: "Perhaps God may give them repentance leading to an accurate knowledge of truth, and they may come back to their proper senses out from the snare of the Devil." (2 Tim. 2:24-26) How fine it would be to have a part in teaching such a person, and thus aiding him to become a praiser of Jehovah!

Your own personal conduct, both in the field ministry and as you go about other activities of life, can often do much to overcome the prejudice of observers and open their minds to the truth. So, it is vital to watch your speech and your deportment at all times, to be sure that they befit a servant of Jehovah God. (1 Pet. 2:12; 3:1, 2) Your personal appearance when participating in the field service should always be one of neatness and cleanliness. Your words, too, if always spoken in a kindly way, will favorably impress right-hearted persons. There is no doubt about it; good results will be forthcoming if we always keep in mind the scripture that says: "In no way are we giving any cause for stumbling, that our ministry might not be found fault with; but in every way we recommend ourselves as God's ministers." —2 Cor. 6:3, 4.

No matter where you may live or what the conditions under which you serve, never lose sight of your personal responsibility as a minister of God. (1 Cor. 9:16) Jehovah has had recorded in his Word examples and advice to encourage us to press on even under the most difficult circumstances. It sets a pattern for us to follow. For example, in the book of Acts we learn that, when our Christian brothers were experiencing official persecution, they did not fearfully cease meeting together for worship, though they did take certain precautions to avoid unnecessary difficulties. (Acts 12:1-17) Threatened by government officials, they did not agree to cease preaching. (Acts 4:18-20; 5:27-32) When circumstances isolated them from their fellow believers, they did not become inactive. (Acts 8:4) Even when imprisoned, they took advantage of opportunities to preach. (Acts 16:25-34; 28:16-31) Jehovah was always close to them; they could pray to him for his spirit, and so can you.—Luke 11:13.

The ministry entrusted to us by God is urgent. Timothy, a faithful servant of God, was helped to appreciate that when he was admonished by a member of the early Christian governing body: "I solemnly charge you before God and Christ Jesus, who is destined to judge the living and the dead, and by his manifestation and his kingdom, preach the word, be at it urgently in favorable season, in troublesome season." (2 Tim. 4:1, 2) How much more urgent it is today, now that the Kingdom is already established and the "last days" of the wicked system of things are coming rapidly to their close! Our "keeping close in mind the presence of the day of Jehovah" will stir us to "deeds of godly devotion" in full measure. (2 Pet. 3:11, 12) This is no time for anyone to render to Jehovah merely "token service," feeling that as long as one spends some time in the field service, that is all that is necessary. It is a time for zeal in the ministry, participating to the full extent that one's circumstances permit.

Never lose sight of the fact that this generation is faced with the impending destruction of Babylon the Great, the world empire of false religion, as well as the Armageddon destruction of all others who have not taken their stand on Jehovah's side. (Rev. 18:2-8; 19:11-21) Only 'those who call on the name of Jehovah will be saved.' However, the Scriptures ask: "How will they call on him in whom they have not put faith? How, in turn, will they put faith in him of whom they have not heard? How, in turn, will they hear without someone to preach?" (Rom. 10:13, 14) Yes, the salvation of other people is influenced by your ministry. (1 Tim. 4:16; Ezek. 3:17-21) Even when the people refuse to listen, the urgency of the work does not diminish. Repeatedly Jehovah has directed his faithful servants to keep on talking. "You must speak my words to them, regardless of whether they hear or they refrain." (Ezek. 2:7; Isa. 6:9) Whether they listen in faith or not, it is our privilege to speak out in behalf of God, to make known his name, to publicize his righteousness and to declare his love. So, with appreciation for what Jehovah has done for you, make your own ministry a reflection of the depth of your love for him.—Isa. 12:4, 5; Ps. 71:14-16; 1 John 4:9-11; 2 Cor. 5:14, 15.

TERRITORY IN WHICH TO PREACH

In order that the ministry may be carried on in an orderly and effective manner, it is both practical and Scriptural for there to be assignments of territory in which to preach. (2 Cor. 10:13; Gal. 2:9) So the Society assigns a certain section of territory to each congregation of Jehovah's witnesses. It is the responsibility of the congregation to see to it that this territory is worked thoroughly just as many times each year as possible. All the territory—cities, towns and rural areas—ought to be given regular attention, and this is done under the supervision of the congregation organization. It is hoped that it can all be covered at least every four months. When frequent calls are made, people are moved to give more serious consideration to the Kingdom message and the interest of sheeplike ones can be stimulated more rapidly. For this reason, congregations that cover their territory more frequently are usually the ones that have the greatest increase.

To facilitate orderly coverage of the congregation's territory, it is divided up locally into smaller sections for assignment to service groups and to individual publishers of the Kingdom. If you would like to have one of these sections of territory assigned to you, the magazine-territory servant will be glad to provide it for you. Although you will probably find that a section close to your home is most convenient, you are welcome to take out one anywhere in the congregation's territory if someone else does not already have it. This, then, becomes your personal territory, and those who live in it are the ones to whom it is your responsibility to minister. With deep love for Jehovah and loving concern for the sheeplike ones, care for it well.—1 Thess. 2:8, 9.

Endeavor to reach the occupants of every home with the good news, if at all possible. This will call for patient perseverance. First of all, as you work in the territory keep a careful record of every place where people are not at home; then try again at another time. If they still are not at home, you may want to put a tract under their door, but keep on trying to make personal contact. Some publishers, after trying several times without finding anyone at home, write a letter in which they give a witness to the householder; or they may arrange for a publisher who is confined to home, due to illness or age, to write such letters.

In addition to private homes, there may be apartments, business establishments and other buildings in your territory. Call on them all. If you cannot get into certain apartments, ask the doorman if you may leave handbills or tracts with him for each of the occupants; or perhaps you can copy down their names and write them personal letters. At convenient times, arrange to call at stores and other business establishments in your territory. The owner may be someone that you will seldom find at his home; and, with his permission, you may be able to talk briefly with his employees too. As you work through your territory again and again, be alert to observe where more than one family lives in a house and where rooms are rented. Keep in mind, too, that there are usually a number of persons in each household, and by working the territory at different times or on different days you may be able to meet various members of the family. Recognizing that the message you carry means life to those who embrace it, be diligent to give everyone in your territory the opportunity to hear it.—John 17:3.

Before you work a section of territory, always be sure that it has been assigned to you. This will help to avoid confusion, as well as needless irritation of householders, and will result in consistent coverage of all the congregation's assignment.

GROUP WITNESSING

For those who would like to share in the field ministry along with other publishers, the congregation also makes ample provision. Every location where congregation meetings are held is viewed as a rendezvous for field service. Not only the Kingdom Hall but all the places where congregation book studies are held are locations where you can meet with other publishers at various times to go out in group witnessing. For this reason the locations where congregation book studies are held are known as rendezvous for service. Since the one with which you are associated is probably near your home, it will no doubt save travel time for you to work with that group.

Your congregation book study servant will endeavor to arrange for group witnessing at times that are convenient for those associated with the study group. From time to time he may talk to those of you in the group to see just what time you have available that you would like to use for group witnessing, and perhaps some can adjust their schedules to coincide with those of others in order to help them. If some can share in service for an hour or so before the book study, he will be glad to arrange for it. Perhaps several are able to go out another night, whether from house to house, making back-calls or conducting home Bible studies; if so, your local book study servant will be glad to make arrangements, even though not everyone is able to do so. Likewise, provision can be made for a group to meet on certain weekdays, if that fits their needs. So, too, many may be able to go out in the field ministry on weekends, while that may not be possible for others. These arrangements for group witnessing are for your convenience.

The circumstances of the household where the service rendezvous is located should also be considered. The congregation book studies are usually located at homes where it is possible for the group to meet at certain regular times for service. But there may be times when some get together for service that it would be better to meet in another location, and that can certainly be arranged.

Sometimes when there are only a very few who can share in the service at a particular time, the congregation overseer may arrange to combine several service groups, if this does not make it inconvenient as far as travel is concerned. On special occasions, as a stimulus to the congregation, he may even arrange for everyone to meet for service at the Kingdom Hall, though this is not done on any regular basis.

Local conditions govern the time that it is suitable to begin calling at homes in the territory. Since the habits of the people are not the same everywhere, and the congregation overseer is well acquainted with the way of life of people in the area, he can decide when it is best for the group to start witnessing from door to door. In some parts of the earth it is possible to engage in field service very early in the day, since that is when people do their work, before it gets too hot. In many localities it is all right to start earlier on weekdays than on Sundays, and that may be done if the circumstances of the publishers also make it possible. But good judgment should always be used.

When you meet with the group for service, by all means put forth a diligent effort to be on time. Usually there is a brief discussion that is designed to help equip you for the service to be done, and you will not want to miss it. At most morning meetings for service (and sometimes, at afternoon meetings), the one serving as chairman of the group will conduct a helpful discussion of the day's text. Then there will be comments on how to approach the people in the territory, what to say, how to overcome objections, how to present the literature or start Bible studies, or something else of practical value in connection with the work that the group will be doing. At times there may be encouraging experiences related. Arrangements will also be made so that everyone knows where he is to work. Of course, it is always appropriate to ask Jehovah's blessing on our efforts to serve him, and this is done before the meeting for service is dismissed. This entire program is usually limited to fifteen minutes, and then you will want to get into the territory just as soon as possible.

If the group meets for service at night, when time is limited, or immediately following a regular congregation meeting, a shorter session is ordinarily arranged. But service arrangements for those in the group are made and prayer is offered, provided they gather at a place where this is possible.

The book study servant will always hold territory in which you can work. Generally this will be reasonably close to the service rendezvous, because it will save travel time and make it convenient to follow through on any interest located. So, when you meet with the group for service, you can obtain from him a portion of territory that is sufficient for the day. Take the same keen interest in covering it thoroughly as you would in your own personal territory, but be sure to let your book study servant know how much you cover, because he is responsible to see that it is all worked before it is turned back to the magazine-territory servant.

If there are quite a number that gather for service at certain times, the book study servant may divide them into two or three smaller groups and ask one to take charge of each group. Should you be requested to care for such a group from time to time, bear in mind that more is involved than simply leading them to the territory. Much

of the effectiveness of the work will depend on
your oversight. If possible, assign sufficient territory to the individuals in the group to keep
them busy for the entire time that they plan to
share in the house-to-house work, so they will not
have to stand around waiting for a further assignment. In localities where territory is scattered,
perhaps you can arrange for just a few to work
in the sparsely settled area while the others concentrate on the more densely populated sections.
If some of the service time is going to be spent
making back-calls, be sure that this is also well
organized. Some may have calls that need to be
made early, and plan to join in the house-to-house
work later. Others may plan to make back-calls
after their house-to-house activity. Inquire ahead
of time as to their plans so that you can cooperate
with them. Remember, too, that your zealous
example, staying out in the service for the full
time period that has been planned, will encourage
the others to do the same.—1 Pet. 5:2, 3.

Group witnessing is especially beneficial for
those who are new publishers of the Kingdom, as
it gives them opportunity to go with someone else
for training. This makes it possible for them to
observe how experienced ones carry on the ministry and to receive helpful counsel and suggestions
as they walk along between houses. Jesus set the
example in this, providing personal training for
his apostles; and, later, when he sent out seventy
other disciples to preach, he arranged for them
to work two by two for a time. (Luke 8:1; 10:1)
In the years that followed, the Christian congregation continued to appreciate the importance of
training those who joined their ranks. (Eph. 4:11,
12) If you feel the need for such training, do not
hesitate to ask for it. The congregation overseer
is keenly interested in seeing that all new publishers are properly trained in the ministry, and
he will be glad to arrange for you to go along

in the service with one of the mature ministers. Your congregation book study servant will also be pleased to help. In fact, since he is right there in the service rendezvous with which you associate, he will gladly arrange for you to work with someone else for training whenever you want to benefit from the assistance available.

As you receive training in the ministry, apply yourself earnestly to make progress, knowing that it will enable you to be a more effective praiser of Jehovah. Prepare well before you go out in the service; and when you have an appointment to work with another publisher, be sure to show appreciation for it by being there. When you learn to do one feature of the service well, seek training in the others too. Work toward the goal of being qualified to assist in training others; you will find added joy when you are able to share in this fine privilege of service.

Even when you become an experienced publisher, you may want to work a few doors with another capable publisher on occasion, with a view to improving the effectiveness of your ministry. But, unless instruction is being given to one who desires help, those who are able to go to the doors alone usually find that much more can be accomplished in this way in the time that they have available for service. They are encouraged as they see other publishers working across the street or down the block from them, but they know that more can be done when they go to the doors by themselves. Nevertheless, at night and in dangerous neighborhoods it may be wise for two publishers to work very close to each other or in pairs.

So there are advantages to be had in group witnessing. When you find it convenient to work with a group, it will be mutually upbuilding. On the other hand, there may be times when you will find that it is advantageous to work alone, and it is quite all right to do that.

PREACHING FROM HOUSE TO HOUSE

The principal means by which "this good news of the kingdom" is being "preached in all the inhabited earth for a witness to all the nations" is house-to-house preaching. (Matt. 24:14) Jesus Christ and his apostles set the example for us in this. Having been instructed by Jesus in the best ways to carry out the ministry, the apostles kept up their house-to-house preaching after the holy spirit came upon them at Pentecost, 33 C.E. Of them, Acts 5:42 reports: "Every day in the temple and from house to house they continued without letup teaching and declaring the good news about the Christ, Jesus." Years later, the apostle Paul reminded mature Christian brothers from Ephesus of the work that he had done in their city, saying: "I did not hold back from telling you any of the things that were profitable nor from teaching you publicly and from house to house." (Acts 20:20) Even today this remains the most effective manner of accomplishing the work. It enables you to come into personal contact with individuals, answer their questions and explain the truth in a way that will be most understandable to them. This is a type of work that fits the capabilities of each one of us, because it involves talking to just one or two persons at a time, and, at the same time, it is the best way to be sure that no one hungering and thirsting for righteousness is overlooked.—Matt. 5:6.

When you start out in the house-to-house work, it is always wise to have something definite in mind to say to the people you meet. It may be just one scripture that you plan to read and discuss, or there may be two or three texts that you are able to tie together in a presentation that is easy to give and easy for others to understand.

Kingdom Ministry regularly offers helpful suggestions. When Jesus preached he emphasized the fact that "the kingdom of the heavens has drawn near," because he, the king, was there among the people. (Matt. 4:17) In our day, too, he said that the Kingdom message would be preached, and appropriately so, because that heavenly government of God is already in operation. So it is always proper to discuss with people how God's kingdom affects their lives and the blessings that it will bring to those who put faith in it. Furthermore, at the conclusion of Jesus' earthly ministry he reported to his Father that he had made the name of God known, and it is appropriate for you, too, as one of Jehovah's witnesses, to make the name of Jehovah prominent by means of your preaching. —John 17:6; Isa. 43:10-12.

To be most effective in your ministry, it is good to learn to be flexible in your presentation. For example, if you observe that there are children in the home, show an interest in them and point out the importance of teaching them the Bible while they are still young. (Matt. 18:2, 3; 19:13-15) If someone has suffered severely due to illness, show why this has been mankind's experience and how the Kingdom will remedy it. (John 9:1-3; Rev. 21:4; Isa. 35:5, 6) When you see evidence that a household is religiously inclined, it may be that you can use this as a springboard to stimulate interest in the message of the Bible. (Acts 17:22-31) In some cases you may find that the particular subject that you had in mind discussing does not appeal to a certain householder, but his remarks may give you a clue as to where his interest does lie. If you have learned several short sermons on a variety of themes, you may be able to adapt to the circumstances and continue the discussion, but along somewhat different lines.—1 Cor. 9:20-23.

Generally you will want to open the Bible and read from it to those you meet, because this impresses others with the fact that the message is not of our own originality but from God. However, among people who do not accept the Bible as God's Word, you may have to talk a little first to help them to see why it is beneficial to consider what the Bible says. In some places publishers find that they are able to accomplish more if they simply carry on a friendly conversation with people, quoting or paraphrasing scriptures in a natural way, and not taking out the Bible actually to read from it until the householder is in a sufficiently receptive frame of mind. Regardless of the method used, though, it is to God's Word the Bible that we always direct attention. —1 Thess. 2:13; 2 Tim. 3:16.

How long you talk at each door will have to be determined by the circumstances. In some parts of the earth people always seem to be in a great hurry, and they may not manifest much interest; so your presentation may at times be limited to just a minute or two. But even in that length of time you may, in a kindly way, be able to say something that will start the householder to thinking. At other times perhaps you can talk for five or ten minutes, or even longer, if they show keen interest or have questions that they want to have answered. Nevertheless, be careful not to stay so long that they will hesitate to invite you in on another occasion. Of course, when you call on someone who is sincerely busy and asks to be excused, it is considerate to be brief in what you say and perhaps to arrange to call again later in the day, or at some other convenient time. The customs of the people among whom you work will also influence the length of your calls. If the people are by nature hospitable and expect to exchange a few friendly comments about the weather before discussing the purpose of your call, you will probably find more hearing ears if you do not ignore the custom. At the same time, keep in mind that your time is valuable, and do not stay unnecessarily long with those who really have no interest in God's Word.

To assist you in the ministry, the Society provides printed material—Bibles, books, booklets, magazines and tracts—to be left with interested persons. Feel free to use any of these items, at any time, to aid others to learn the truth. Of course, each month a suggestion is made in *Kingdom Ministry* as to the literature offer to be featured in the field service, and it is beneficial to follow this suggestion. The Society's printing plants are geared to provide you with this literature at the time designated, and the service meeting program is specially arranged to aid you to handle it effectively. The information in the literature being featured is vital for the public, and we want to make it available to everyone possible. However, when you meet someone who already has this literature, or some other circumstances make it advisable, do not hesitate to make good use of the other publications that have been provided.

As you call from house to house, it is recommended that you keep a careful record both of those who are not at home and of those who manifest interest. Then call back. Remember, as Jesus instructed his apostles, when you carry on your ministry in a territory you are to "search out who in it is deserving" so that you can spend further time with them to build up their faith and aid them to be numbered among those who make known the greatness of our God.—Matt. 10:11; Ps. 145:6; Deut. 32:3.

It may be that sometime in your house-to-house work someone will ask you for an identification. As far as any authorization to do the work is concerned, this you have from God, as we have already seen from the Scriptures, and we do not ask men for permission to do God's work. (Acts 5:27-32) However, a simple identification card signed by the congregation overseer is helpful at times, and this can be obtained on request. Such cards are issued to any dedicated and baptized publisher who regularly engages in house-to-house witnessing and is able to call at homes by himself and give an effective witness.

BACK-CALLS

When, in the house-to-house work, you find someone who manifests interest in the Scriptures, it is wise to call back on that person. Your commission, as stated by Jesus, is to "make disciples of people . . . teaching them to observe all the things I have commanded you." (Matt. 28:19, 20) That cannot possibly be accomplished on just one visit. It requires repeated calls to cultivate the interest, clear out obstacles and aid the newly interested ones to get a firm grip on the Word of life.

The making of back-calls should be a prominent part of your ministry, and you will find that, if you regularly participate in the house-to-house work and keep a careful record of those who show interest, you will always have back-calls to make. Some, while refusing to take literature for various reasons, may listen to what you say and show interest in the Scriptures. Why not call back and see if you can further that interest? Others may accept only a tract, but some fine home Bible studies have been started as a result of following through on such calls. When a subscription for *The Watchtower* or *Awake!* is obtained, it is always advantageous to call back and deliver the current issue, until the magazine starts to come through the mail, and to use this opportunity to talk a little more about the kingdom of God. Likewise, if a name has been received by the congregation with the request that someone call, and this information is turned over to you, faithfully give it your attention. Back-calls should also be made on all who accept books, booklets or magazines, because they have manifested a willingness to give further consideration to the things about which you talked. It is true that a few of these persons may have shown only slight interest, but what they read may change their entire viewpoint. "The word of God is alive and exerts power," and it is that word that is discussed in all the literature that we offer in our ministry. (Heb. 4:12) There are many persons who showed only a little interest at first who are now zealous publishers—because someone called back.

Keep in mind that we are endeavoring to search out those who manifest sheeplike qualities and aid them to get into the fold, where they can enjoy the loving care of our Great Shepherd Jehovah God and his Fine Shepherd Jesus Christ. (Ezek. 34:11-14, 31; John 10:11, 16; Rev. 7:16, 17) When a shepherd locates a lost sheep, hurt and hungry, he does not leave it unattended, content simply that he knows where it is. He gives it tender personal care, providing it with food and water just as soon as possible, to build up its strength. Our concern for these potential praisers of Jehovah will move us to care for them just as diligently.—Matt. 9:36-38.

After you locate someone in the territory who displays sheeplike qualities, it is usually beneficial to call again soon—if possible, within a week. In this way you may be able to keep alive the interest that was shown on your earlier call.

When you make your back-calls, be friendly and natural. Rather than giving an extended speech, allow the householder opportunity to share in the conversation. Do not feel that you have to know the answer to every question that people may ask; you are simply there to share with them good things that you have learned.—Mark 5:18-20.

Of course, you will accomplish the most good on your calls if you have in mind something definite to say. By way of preparation you might locate a few more scriptures on the topic that interested the householder on your previous visit. For some calls, you could select a few paragraphs in one of the Society's publications that you would like to read and discuss together. Then, as you cover the information with the householder, suggest that he get his own Bible, if he has one, and look up the references with you. Generally this makes a very favorable impression, as he may be surprised to see the things that you are saying right in his copy of the Bible.

At first the people on whom you call may listen somewhat passively to what you say; but when they start asking questions, it is wise to realize that those questions are the key to their interest in continued discussions. If you know the Scriptural answers, do not hesitate to change from your prepared presentation to answer them. And if they ask something that you are not equipped to handle then, simply tell them that you will see what you can find out about it and will discuss it when you call again. Patiently help them to realize that the problems and questions that they are most concerned about in life are answered in the Bible. In time you may be able to conduct a regular home Bible study with them.

You will often find that considerable patience is required to stimulate a person's spiritual growth. (Jas. 5:7) He may be disillusioned by the hypocrisy of the false religious leaders and, for that reason, somewhat skeptical even of your reason for calling. On the other hand, he may encounter pressure from acquaintances and relatives to turn him away from the truth. Others may be so busy trying to satisfy material wants and needs that they cannot seem to find time to sit down and discuss the Scriptures. With your patient care, it may be that these obstacles can be cleared away so that the person can begin to grow spiritually. In this work it is our privilege to be fellow workers with God; for while it is our assignment to plant and water, it is God who causes growth.—1 Cor. 3:6-9; Luke 8:11-15.

For your participation in this important work to be most productive of good results, you will find it beneficial to share in it on a regular basis. It is suggested that you set aside some of your service time each week to call back on interested persons that you have already located. If you are working in the same territory week after week, whether alone or with a group, you will find it convenient to make these calls, because they will be right in the vicinity where you are working. Some may choose to make their calls during the daytime; others find that they get good results in the evening. You may share in this work at any time that is convenient. But do not leave it to chance; plan your back-call activity.

HOME BIBLE STUDIES

If you are diligent in the field service, showing keen interest in those to whom you preach, in time you will probably have the joy of conducting a home Bible study. This is the foremost means by which persons are aided to come to an accurate knowledge of the truth. It is God's will that all kinds of men gain such knowledge, and you can have a part in helping them to do so. (1 Tim. 2:3, 4) As those with whom you study progress in spiritual growth and their lives begin to change, your heart will overflow with gratitude to Jehovah for the privilege of having part in such a work. And when they become devoted servants of God along with you, you will feel as did the apostle Paul, who said to some persons that he had helped to learn the Word of God: "What is our hope or joy or crown of exultation—why, is it not in fact you?— . . . You certainly are our glory and joy."—1 Thess. 2:13, 19, 20.

Make it your goal to conduct at least one home Bible study each week. If you have children with whom you can conduct such a study, by all means do so. But, in addition to that, endeavor to arrange for a study with someone in another household, so that he, too, can benefit from the good things that you are able to share with him. Of course, if you are able to care for more than one study, then you will find that your rewards of joy will increase accordingly.

Bible studies can be started in a variety of ways. Many publishers have had good results in starting studies when making their very first call on a person, in house-to-house work. They simply say that their purpose in calling is to assist their neighbors to understand the Bible and that they would be pleased to study the Bible with the householder or the entire family at a convenient time each week at no cost. Others give a sermon first, and then, if interest is manifested, offer to demonstrate how to make a study of the Scriptures both informative and enjoyable. Frequently studies are started when a back-call is made, simply by using the Society's publications, along with the Bible, as a source of answers to the householders' questions. At first the person may not even realize that he is having a home Bible study; he just enjoys the fine Bible discussions. In many parts of the world it is necessary to make a number of calls, discussing a variety of topics and answering questions, before it is possible to get down to a regular study. The important thing is to help the interested person to spend some time on a regular basis discussing God's Word. If at all possible, when you get a study started, arrange for it to be held each week for a full hour.

What publication will you use for your study? Do not hesitate to start with any chapter or any article in any of the Society's publications, if that is what is needed to hold the interest of the householder. If you find that you personally are better able to use the presentation of a topic as set out in one of the publications than you are another, that is all right. They have all been prepared for your use. With some persons it is necessary to use just their Bible for several weeks to win their confidence before you direct their attention to the study aids provided by the Watch Tower Bible and Tract Society. Others readily accept the use of the Society's publications along with the Bible.

There is no arbitrary ruling as to how the study should be conducted, but be sure that the student really understands the points discussed. We recommend that you urge the student to study the lesson before you come, perhaps even demonstrating how to do this. In this way it will be possible to ask the questions on the paragraphs, look up the scriptures that are cited, and then read the material in the paragraph as a summary. When the study is new, you may find it beneficial to look up all the scriptures, whether they are quoted in the publication or not. In this way you focus principal attention on the Bible itself. But after a short time, it should be possible simply to discuss what the texts quoted in the paragraphs say, while looking up those that are cited but not quoted. This will enable you to make greater headway. Right from the start it is certainly appropriate for you to seek Jehovah's blessing regularly before you go to conduct the study. However, you will have to determine when the student is properly adjusted religiously to show him the importance of prayer to Jehovah through Christ in connection with the study. Then it would be appropriate to open your study each week with prayer, asking Jehovah's blessing, and to conclude with a prayer of thanksgiving for the fine things learned.—Ps. 25:4; Jas. 1:5; Eph. 5:20.

As we have already noted, it is our privilege to be "fellow workers" with God by sharing in the ministry. The apostle Paul had a prominent share in such work. He was called to be an heir of the heavenly kingdom with Christ, and he was used in gathering and preparing others for that high calling. He did not teach in such a way as to draw attention to himself or cause others to look to him as their leader. (1 Cor. 1:13-15; 2:1-5; 3:5-7; Matt. 23:10) He always directed attention to Jehovah God and to His provision for salvation through His Son Jesus Christ. In harmony with God's declared will, he laid Christ as a foundation by teaching the truth about him and aiding others to make belief in that truth part of their own lives. Furthermore, he stressed that building that was done on that foundation ought to be of fire-resistant materials, with characteristics like those of gold, silver and precious stones. That is, durable Christian qualities had to be built into the individual being instructed in God's Word; otherwise, all that spiritual building work would be destroyed when subjected to fiery trial. (1 Cor. 3:10-15) Surely no one would want that to happen to his work.

Those same principles of building that applied to the work done by Paul and his associates in connection with prospective members of the body of Christ also apply to the work in which you are privileged to share today. Those that you teach need more than to be able to answer certain questions on basic doctrinal matters. Rather, as Paul wrote to those whom he had taught: "You should be made new in the force actuating your mind, and should put on the new personality which was created according to God's will in true righteousness and loyalty." (Eph. 4:23, 24) Gaining accurate knowledge is a necessary part of putting on this new personality with its many durable qualities. The needed changes just do not take place when a person does not understand a matter clearly. So, patiently explain matters to those with whom you study and draw them out with questions to be sure they understand.—Col. 3:10.

As you study with them, help them to see the Scriptural reasons for things that are said. Encourage them to incorporate scriptures in their answers and to seek out Bible principles when decisions must be made. In this way inculcate deep regard for Scriptural principles and reliance on Jehovah God.—Prov. 3:5, 6.

When reading Bible accounts that draw attention to either desirable or undesirable qualities, emphasize Jehovah's view of the situation. Patiently endeavor to cultivate a desire on their part to be pleasing to Jehovah in everything.—Ps. 19:13, 14.

Rather than endeavoring simply to cover a large amount of material at each home Bible study, pause at appropriate points to build appreciation. (Ps. 27:4) In that way you build up the spiritual heart of both yourself and the ones that you are teaching. (Prov. 4:23) As opportunity affords, highlight the grand qualities of Jehovah God as manifest in his works and purposes, so helping the students to draw closer to God. Inculcate deep respect for Jehovah's wisdom so that they will readily respond to the direction of his Word. Magnify his justice, to fortify them against the onslaughts of skeptics. Help them to know Jehovah as one who loves his servants and cares for them and to whom they can turn with confidence. (1 John 4:10; Matt. 6:25-34) In this way work toward developing in them a strong feeling of devotion and loyalty toward Jehovah. If they truly know Jehovah and love his ways, they will never forsake his service or become indifferent about his will for them.—1 Chron. 28:9.

Something else that they need to be taught, a little at a time, is appreciation for Jehovah's organization. This can be done in a natural way, because when you talk about the things that you have been doing and enjoying, you will be telling them about the congregation meetings, assemblies, and so forth. Gradually explain to them how the organization functions. When considering various aspects of the organization, you may want to emphasize the Scriptural reason for things; on another occasion, you may stress how a certain thing marks Jehovah's people as different from the world; at other times you may highlight the great joy that we find in doing Jehovah's will. There may be times when you discuss something about the organization before your study, or perhaps afterward. On certain weeks the study material itself may give rise to additional remarks about the congregation.

As soon as it seems to be appropriate, invite the newly interested ones to go along with you to the congregation book study or other congregation meetings. To put them at ease, you might explain in advance how the meeting is conducted, that no collections are taken and that they will not be called on to say anything unless they want to raise their hand and offer a comment. When they respond to your invitation, introduce them to others at the meeting and make them feel welcome. At the Kingdom Hall, explain the congregation activity and progressively acquaint them with the servants and the services that they perform. Do not be satisfied with merely telling them a little about the organization. Over a period of time, put forth an earnest effort to help them to know it well, to appreciate it as Jehovah's and to feel gratitude for the privilege of associating with it and having a share in its activity.

As you study together week after week, keep in mind that the home Bible study is not the end in itself. It has as its purpose the producing of additional praisers of Jehovah God. So the students need to be helped to think in terms of using what they learn. As Proverbs 4:7 says: "Wisdom is the prime thing. Acquire wisdom." Wisdom, here referred to, is the ability to use knowledge in a right way. In tactful ways direct attention to such right use of what is being learned. You may spend a little extra time discussing scriptures that refer to the preaching work. Some questions might be phrased in such a way that the student is made to think in terms of explaining the matter to his friends. Perhaps you will relate some of your own field experiences or read some fitting ones from the *Yearbook* at times. When they attend the congregation meetings, they will hear more discussion of the field service and arrangements that are made for it. Gradually their desire to share in this grand privilege of service will grow, and, when they qualify to go along in the field service, it can be your happy privilege to instruct them in this too.

In determining how long to continue studying with a person, you must consider the circumstances. At first some householders may welcome you largely because they like to have you visit with them, and not because of keen interest in the truth. But this friendliness may open the way for them to see and appreciate God's loving purposes. However, if, after a time, the person does not manifest any real progress, then it may be that you could spend the time more advantageously on other calls. On the other hand, if the householder gives evidence of appreciation of the things being learned, and shows some measure of progress, you will want to continue to help him to grow in knowledge, in love and in appreciation of the privilege of serving Jehovah God.

(Phil. 1:9-11) Help him to become a mature Christian. Even after he starts out in the field service, yes, even after dedication and baptism, it is usually advisable to continue the study for a time until he gets well established in the way of the truth.

The Lord Jesus, shortly before returning to his Father in heaven, emphasized the importance of this kind, personal attention to persons with sheeplike traits. He spoke of those whom he called "lambs" and "little sheep," persons whose spiritual growth was just beginning, and urged that they be tenderly cared for, as a shepherd cares for the young in his flock. By a series of three questions to the apostle Peter, Jesus impressed the point that willingness to share in this activity is in reality a demonstration of our love for Christ. —John 21:15-17.

Who qualifies to share in this feature of service? You do! Remember, God does not give us the whole job to do ourselves. He simply invites us to be his fellow workers. We plant and water, but it is God who makes it grow. Even if you have much education and can speak persuasively, this will not make persons whose hearts are not right accept the good news. On the other hand, publishers with very limited worldly education have studied with well-read persons, and with good results. Their very willingness to conduct such a study, along with their obvious sincerity and love for God, has deeply impressed right-hearted householders, who, as a result, have joined them in making known Jehovah's praises. Publishers who are physically blind conduct studies by having the householder or another publisher do the reading. Some even study with persons who read another language, having the householder do all the reading and then discussing the points together to the extent possible. They appreciate the importance of aiding others to learn the truth now, while there is yet time. They are *willing* to serve Jehovah in this way. Are you? Then you, too, can have a share.

MAGAZINE DISTRIBUTION

Another method of preaching the good news of the Kingdom is through the distribution of the magazines *The Watchtower* and *Awake!* This activity accomplishes much good. It enables us to get the Kingdom message into the hands of those who have even limited interest. Though they may not listen to a sermon at the door, and they may not want a larger piece of literature, they are often willing to accept the magazines with their short articles. And what about others in the home who pick them up? Although we may never have met them personally to give a witness, the magazines can help to do the job.

The Watchtower faithfully directs the attention of all who read it toward Jehovah's kingdom. Each issue contains articles that are designed to be specially appealing and beneficial to the public, as well as material for more advanced Bible students. *Awake!*, which is also published in many languages, is designed with a broad coverage of practical and informative articles that often appeal to persons who are not inclined to read our other publications. Tactfully it helps them to appreciate how Bible principles should affect one's view on all the various matters of life and it stimulates their desire for more Bible knowledge. Both magazines have aided many persons to break free from the bondage in which Satan holds mankind. —2 Tim. 2:24-26; 1 John 5:19.

If possible, spend some time in the distribution of the magazines each week. You will find it beneficial, and most productive of good results, to have a regular time set aside for this activity. Your congregation no doubt features this work as the principal activity one day a week, and you may be able to participate in it then. If not, feel free to do it at any convenient time.

When engaging in this feature of service, you will find that a very brief presentation is usually sufficient. Simply draw attention to an article that you believe will specially appeal to the individual and then offer the magazines on the regular contribution. Often your presentation will be less than a minute in length. But, of course, our goal is not simply the placement of magazines; we are searching for the "sheep," and, if someone shows keen interest, you may want to talk a little more and then arrange for a back-call.

Magazines may be distributed by calling from house to house, as well as by making brief calls at business places and approaching people on the street. Why, anytime that you are walking from one place to another or shopping or waiting for a bus, you may offer the current magazines to the people you meet. Additionally, when engaging in any other feature of the service, magazines may be offered, and to good advantage.

It is a good idea to call back on those who obtain magazines from you. Especially where unusual interest was found on the first call is it wise to return soon to cultivate that interest by Bible discussion. Many fine home Bible studies have developed from return calls on magazine placements. Return visits on others who accepted the magazines, perhaps in two weeks with the new issues, will also be appreciated by some of them, and in this way you can develop a regular magazine route. Your share in distributing the magazines will help to keep the Kingdom message prominently before the people in your territory.

OTHER WITNESSING

Being a minister of God, you will want to be ready and willing at all times to share a knowledge of his grand purposes with others. This is something that can be done, not only when you are in the house-to-house work or some other regular feature of the ministry, but at any time. When traveling on trains and buses, during lunch time at work or school, when deliverymen and others call at your door and when you meet a neighbor in the garden, there are golden opportunities to give a witness. You may want to carry some Bible tracts with you for use on such occasions.

Do not forget your relatives. They, too, need the Kingdom hope. When Andrew of Bethsaida learned the identity of the Messiah, the first one that he told about it was his brother Simon. (John 1:35-42) Later, when Simon Peter was sent to give a witness to Cornelius in Caesarea, he found that Cornelius had enthusiastically "called together his relatives and intimate friends," and they, too, accepted the truth. (Acts 10:24, 44) How fine it would be if you could help some of your relatives in a similar way!

In witnessing to others while going about the customary activities of life Jesus set a fine example. When pausing for water at a well in Samaria, he used a woman's question as an opening for a fine discussion of spiritual matters, and quite a number from that vicinity believed in him as a result. (John 4:5-42) In your everyday life, too, you will find that others frequently raise sincere questions or express concern about world conditions, and you can follow through by pointing to the Bible's high moral standard and the Kingdom hope. Furthermore, if you talk freely about the meetings you attend, the student talks you give, the things you read, and so forth, this may bring a response and open the way to discuss other spiritual matters. You will find that your personal acquaintances and relatives are usually more willing to discuss matters freely with you than with a Witness they do not know who knocks on their door. Use this opening to good advantage, and for their lasting benefit.

Aged and infirm publishers, and even those who may simply be confined to their homes for a few days due to illness, can do a great deal of preaching by means of the telephone, letter writing and talking with the people who visit them. If our hearts are full and overflowing with appreciation for the good things that God has done, it will not be difficult to find opportunities to talk.

CHAPTER 5

Reporting Your Field Ministry

THE Society, as well as the local congregation, is keenly interested in knowing what is being accomplished in the field ministry month by month and year by year. Such a record provides encouragement to all of us, it serves as a guide in providing spiritual aid to those who need it and it makes possible the orderly oversight of the preaching work. (Acts 2:41; 4:4; 8:14; 2 Cor. 10: 13) So we request that all of Jehovah's witnesses make weekly reports to their congregation of what they have done by way of preaching the good news to others.

At the Kingdom Hall you can get a supply of report slips, designed for you to make a daily note of your preaching activity. At the end of each week, total the figures on it and put it in the report box that is provided. When making out your reports, have the following points in mind:

"Books": In this column on the report slip show the total number that you personally placed with any persons who are not baptized witnesses of Jehovah, as well as with any who, although baptized, have not reported field service for at least six months. Count all books printed by the Society, including Bibles. (If you occasionally provide some literature to another congregation publisher for distribution in the field service, this should not be included in your report.)

"Booklets": Total number placed with persons who are not baptized witnesses of Jehovah, as well as with any who, although baptized, have not reported field service for at least six months.

"Hours in Field Service": Time spent preaching God's Word to persons who are not baptized witnesses of Jehovah, counting from when you personally make your first call in the territory until you leave your last call. If two publishers are working together, both may count the time, as long as both share in giving the witness. Time used in giving a witness to those who visit your home or to people at any other place may be included in your report. Time spent writing letters to give a witness concerning God's kingdom may also be counted. Additionally, time may be reported when it is spent in conducting a home Bible study with one's own unbaptized children or when it is used for giving instruction to anyone else who, though he may share in field service, has not yet been baptized. The same is true of time spent in actually conducting a home Bible study with another publisher who, even though baptized, is *both* irregular in field service (missing entire months in field service) and seldom attends congregation meetings. Likewise, time spent in making calls on anyone who, though baptized, has not reported field service for at least six months may be counted as hours in the field service if God's Word is discussed and the person is encouraged to come back to meetings. (This time spent in teaching baptized persons, when circumstances require it, may be reported until such time as they again report field service for two consecutive months and start attending meetings.)

Public speakers may count the time spent in actually delivering any public talk.

"New *Watchtower* and *Awake!* Subscriptions": Total number obtained as new subscriptions from persons who are not baptized witnesses of Jehovah, as well as from any who, although baptized, have not reported field service for at least six months.

"Individual Magazines": Total number placed with persons who are not baptized witnesses of Jehovah, as well as with any who, although baptized, have not reported field service for at least six months.

"Back-Calls": Total number of return calls on persons who are not baptized witnesses of Jehovah but who previously showed some interest in the Kingdom message that you gave them or whose name you were given with the request that you make the call to stimulate further interest. The person who previously showed the interest should be contacted and an effort made to further that one's interest in God's Word. Even if the call is quite brief, either because the person is no longer interested or because it is not a convenient time for him to invite you in, it may be reported. The visit should have been made with the intention of making a back-call. If two publishers go together, only one will report the back-call. Back-calls may also be reported when a letter is written to give a further witness to a person who has already responded to the Kingdom message, or when the additional witness is given over the telephone. The call may likewise be counted if you deliver to an interested person a piece of literature, as on a magazine route, or if you call an unbaptized person on the phone to invite him to a meeting or stop at his home to take him with you to a congregation meeting. If you call on an unbaptized publisher to invite that one to go in the service with you or to take him along in service with you that day, it may be reported as a back-call, since the one on whom you are calling is not yet an ordained minister. A back-call is to be reported each time you conduct a home Bible study with anyone who is not yet baptized, and with any who, even though baptized, are *both* irregular in field service (missing entire months in field service) and seldom attend congregation meetings. Back-calls may also be counted for calls made to give spiritual assistance to persons who, although baptized, have not reported field service for at least six months.

"Bible Study Report": At the end of each month please fill out a Bible Study Report for every study conducted, whether with an individual or a family group. Always include yourself as the conductor in the attendance figure. New studies are not to be reported in this way until they have been held twice after the call on which the study arrangement was first demonstrated, or a total of three times, and there is reason to believe that the study will continue. Studies conducted with anyone who is not a baptized witness of Jehovah should be reported until he is baptized. There may also be persons who, although baptized, seldom come to the congregation meetings *and* are irregular in reporting any field service (missing entire months in field service); or perhaps they have become inactive, reporting no field service for at least six months. If you can start a regular study with such a person, you may include this activity in your report of field service. You may report both the home Bible study and the time spent in conducting the study, helping the person to get restored to Jehovah's organization. Such a study may be reported until such time as the person again goes out in the field service for two consecutive months and starts to attend meetings. After this, of course, it is wise to continue to encourage the individual to keep feeding on the spiritual food provided at congregation meetings, and more personal assistance may be needed, but you will no longer report the home Bible study even though you continue to conduct it for a while longer because of your loving concern for your dedicated brother or sister.

Obviously, these reports of your field service do not include everything that you do as a minister of God. For example, your personal study, attending of meetings, visiting the sick and needy, studying with newly baptized ones, traveling to and from the territory where you preach, caring for the Kingdom Hall and other responsibilities that you may have in the congregation. The fact that you do not report the time spent in these various activities does not mean that they are any less important. To the contrary, all of them are very necessary and part of our lives as servants of Jehovah God. In fact, if we were to report all the time that is involved in our activity as Christians, the report would show twenty-four hours a day, because every aspect of the life of a mature Christian is directly affected by the fact that he is a minister of God. However, on our field service report all that is wanted is what is outlined in the paragraphs above, in connection with taking the good news of the Kingdom to those persons who are not already devoted subjects of Jehovah and his kingdom, to show to what extent the good news of the Kingdom is being preached.

WHO MAY REPORT AS A PUBLISHER?

While you personally qualify to report as a Kingdom publisher, a discussion of this matter will help you to know when it is proper to invite others to go along with you in the Kingdom service. Of course, anyone is free to talk about the things he believes. When his heart is touched by the things he hears from God's Word, he may

be moved to share them with other people, and
that is fine. (Matt. 9:24-26) However, when you
as one of Jehovah's witnesses invite someone to
go along with you from house to house and share
in giving the witness, and so identify him
publicly with the work of Jehovah's witnesses, it
is different. Now he is going to tell people that he
is calling as an associate of Jehovah's witnesses,
and others are going to view him as an example
of what Jehovah's witnesses are. Is he ready for
that?

To determine the answer, consider these points:
Does he believe that the Bible is the inspired
Word of God? (2 Tim. 3:16) Does he know and
believe at least the basic teachings of the Scriptures so that, when asked questions, he will answer in harmony with the Bible, and not according to false religious teachings? (2 Tim. 2:15;
Matt. 7:21-23) Is he heeding the Bible's command
to associate with Jehovah's people in congregation
meetings (if he physically and circumstantially
can)? (Heb. 10:24, 25; Ps. 122:1) Does he apply
in his life what the Bible says about honesty?
(Eph. 4:25, 28) Does he know what the Bible
says about fornication and adultery, and live in
harmony with it? (Heb. 13:4; Matt. 19:9) Does
he heed the Bible's prohibition of drunkenness?
(Eph. 5:18; 1 Pet. 4:3, 4) Has he definitely
broken off membership in all false religious or-
ganizations with which he may have been affili-
ated, and has he ceased attending their meetings
and sharing in their activities? (Rev. 18:4; 2 Cor.
6:14-18) Is he free from any involvement in the
political affairs of the world? (John 6:15; 15:19;
Jas. 1:27) Does he believe and live in harmony
with what the Bible, at Isaiah 2:4, says about
the affairs of the nations? Does he want to be
one of Jehovah's Christian witnesses? (Ps. 110:3)
Before inviting anyone to go along with you in
the field service, it would be wise to discuss these

requirements together. It is not necessary to pry into his life with personal questions, but be sure that he understands that before one has the privilege of sharing in the field service his life must harmonize with these Scriptural requirements. In this way you will not be urging anyone to start out in the service before he is really ready for it.

If the one whom you are training in the field service assists in giving the witness to householders by taking part in the conversation, he, too, may be invited to turn in a field service report, even though he is not yet baptized. It is your privilege to explain to him how and why the reporting is done. But never turn in a report for someone else, unless the other person requests that you do so, possibly due to physical handicap or inability to read and write.

It may be that you are a parent, and, if so, you may take your children out into the field service with you, since it is your responsibility to look after them. Of course, if the children are not really interested in preaching and are just going along because you require it, they should not turn in reports as Kingdom publishers. But if they do show a desire to serve Jehovah, it is beneficial to take them along with you just as often as possible and to train them to share in the work. It will have a far-reaching effect on their lives in the years to come. (Deut. 6:5-7; Prov. 22:6) When one of your children has a knowledge of fundamental Bible truths, really appreciates that what he is doing is service to Jehovah, shows a desire to share in that work regularly and is able to make his own presentation in some feature of the service, at least with the magazines, then you may encourage him to start reporting as a publisher. Have in mind, though, that the responsibility rests upon you as the parent to make arrangements on a regular basis for the child to participate in the service. Do not expect others to carry this load for you. Of course, if the young publisher shows a keen desire to share in the service, it is all right for you to arrange for him to work with other publishers too, if that is agreeable both to you and to them.

YOUR PUBLISHER'S RECORD CARD

Whenever a qualified person begins to preach the good news and reports his activity to the congregation, a Publisher's Record card is made out for him and kept on file by the congregation. On it a record is made each month of the share that he has had in the field service. There is such a Publisher's Record card kept by the congregation for you. It is nothing that is open to examination by everyone else, to compare what he is doing with your report. However, it is consulted from time to time by the servants in the congregation, to determine what assistance, if any, they can offer to you, because they are keenly interested in your spiritual welfare. If you should want to do so, you, too, are welcome to examine your card.

The file of cards is divided into three sections. One contains the cards of those congregation publishers who have made a dedication and symbolized it by water baptism, and so are recognized by the congregation as ordained ministers. A second section is made up of the cards of those publishers who have not yet been baptized but who meet the qualifications to report as publishers and who are being trained to become ministers of God. The third section contains cards for those who are regular or special pioneers in the congregation. When the cards are completely filled, they are put into a permanent file; they are retained for eight years.

Your Publisher's Record card is a record of your ministry. So, if you move to another congregation, be sure to ask your overseer for your current card and all the previous ones on file and then turn them over to the overseer at the Kingdom Hall where you will be attending in the future. If you are going to be away from your home congregation for only a short time, of course, you ought to mail your service reports back regularly. But if you plan to be in a congregation for more than three months, then it is better to take your Publisher's Record cards along to the new congregation.

Those who go out in the field service and turn in a report each month, and who have done so for the past six months, as shown by the Publisher's Record cards, are counted as regular publishers. Any who do not yet have a full six-month record or who have missed any months in the past six are termed irregular publishers. It should be your determination to be a regular publisher of the Kingdom. Certainly anyone who counts it a privilege to serve Jehovah should be able to find some time each month to preach the good news to some other person and aid him to a better understanding of God's Word. These are urgent times in which we live and it is vital that we stay awake spiritually and not allow other cares of life to crowd out our service to God.—Luke 21:34-36.

It is true that some will allow their love for Jehovah to cool off, and they will stop sharing in the preaching of God's kingdom. The servants will do everything they can to assist such individuals, and you too can offer help. (Jas. 5:19, 20) But if such a person becomes completely inactive, not having reported field service for six months, there is no reason to retain his card in the active file of those making up the congregation. We sincerely pray that that will never happen to you, but that strong love for Jehovah will always moti-

vate you and that you will find real joy in serving
God.—Phil. 1:9-11; Ps. 35:9.

THE CONGREGATION REPORT

Each month all the field service reports are
compiled, also the home Bible study reports submitted by congregation publishers are counted,
and a total report of the congregation's activity
is sent to the Society. This report is put in the
mail no later than the fifth day of the month. Of
course, for the report to be complete, your cooperation is required. Your overseer will appreciate
it very much if you turn in your field service reports regularly each week and then if, at the close
of the month, you promptly report any further
activity for the last few days of the month and
turn in your Bible study reports.

When all the reports are received by the Society's branch offices, they are compiled; and a
monthly service report is published in *Kingdom
Ministry* for the benefit of all the congregation.
The annual worldwide report of the preaching
activity of Jehovah's witnesses appears in the
Yearbook of Jehovah's Witnesses, along with in-
teresting field experiences from each country.
But, of course, for such reports to be published
for your encouragement, each publisher of the
Kingdom must report his field service regularly.

There are also figures included in those published reports that you as a publisher do not
supply, but most of them are sent in by your
congregation overseer. For example, on the
monthly report card sent to the Society he shows
the total number of public meetings put on by the
congregation during the month, whether held at
the Kingdom Hall or elsewhere. Funerals are included in this figure. The public meeting held in
connection with the circuit assembly, however, is
reported by the district servant. On occasion,
there may be some who get baptized under the

supervision of the congregation. This, too, is noted on the monthly report card, at the bottom, the overseer showing the total number immersed; and if any were rebaptized, this figure is listed separately. Most individuals who are ready to symbolize their dedication are able to get baptized at circuit or district assemblies, though, and the number is reported by the district servant. As for the attendance at congregation meetings, this is recorded by the one in charge of the meeting and reported on a Study Report slip; then, in time, it is relayed to the Society by the circuit servant. So, as you can see, there are many who cooperate together to make those published reports available for you.

After the report is sent off to the Society, the congregation's service activity is also shown on the information board in the Kingdom Hall for the benefit of everyone associated with the congregation. (Prov. 15:30) This report enables you to see how you are doing in comparison with the congregation as a whole. Thus it serves as a source of encouragement and stimulation to us as individuals, and when certain features of the ministry are in need of special attention by the entire congregation, this is readily apparent. We should all be keenly interested in the congregation report, because it is a reflection of the zeal of the congregation in preaching the Kingdom message, which is a vital part of our lives as Jehovah's witnesses.—Titus 2:13, 14.

It is the earnest hope of everyone associated with the congregation that there will be an increase in the number of active praisers of Jehovah throughout the year; and, of course, if they continue to live in the congregation territory, this increase will be reflected in the congregation report. Special attention is given to this aspect of our work during December and April of each service year. At those times everyone is encouraged to give special thought to those with whom he has been studying the Bible and who are now attending meetings, to see if any of them are ready to start out in the service, and, if they are, we want to help them. So we put forth an extra effort along this line during certain months, and it is a good stimulus to all of us to keep in mind that we are preparing those with whom we study to become active praisers of Jehovah. (2 Tim. 2:1, 2) It is not that we do not start out new publishers during other months; we do. But we have set aside certain times during the year to concentrate on this aspect of our work.

In some places the increases are large, and this is a cause for great rejoicing. (Acts 15:3) Elsewhere, the growth may not be as spectacular, but the faithfulness of those who persevere in Jehovah's service is no less a source of joy to Jehovah and to his people. How much more growth in number of dedicated servants of Jehovah there will be in the years remaining before the end of this wicked system of things, we do not know. But as long as the opportunity is open, we will continue to encourage all who will listen to join us in giving public praise to Jehovah.—Ps. 150:1, 6; Heb. 13:15.

CHAPTER 6

Mature Christian Brothers to Help You

IN THE congregation with which you are associated you will find mature Christian brothers who are glad to be of help to you. They have love for their brothers and are interested in their spiritual welfare. They have taken to heart what Jesus said to his disciples before leaving them: "I am giving you a new commandment, that you love one another; just as I have loved you, that you also love one another. By this all will know that you are my disciples, if you have love among yourselves." (John 13:34, 35; 15:12, 13) While this is true of all who really are Christ's disciples, you will find it manifest in increased measure on the part of those who are spiritually mature. The appointed servants in the congregation are such persons. Because of Christian love for you, the servants may occasionally offer you Scriptural counsel or suggestions in connection with your ministry. You, too, should feel free to approach any of them for assistance or suggestions in connection with your field ministry, assignments you may have on the meetings, questions that arise in your personal study, and other matters in relation to your service to God. To be of service to you and for your convenience, they usually endeavor to get to the Kingdom Hall at least twenty minutes before congregation meetings and stay for a while after the meetings are dismissed.

When Jesus was carrying on his ministry on earth, he said on one occasion: "Come to me, all you who are toiling and loaded down, and I will refresh you . . . for I am mild-tempered and lowly in heart." (Matt. 11:28, 29) Those who accepted his invitation were, indeed, refreshed. When Jesus returned to heaven he did not leave his disciples without loving shepherds to care for them. (Eph. 4:8, 11) Such shepherds endeavor to walk faithfully in the footsteps of their Master; they too endeavor to manifest "lowliness of mind," and in your association with them you will find great spiritual refreshment.—1 Pet. 5:5; Isa. 32:2.

These brothers who are "taking the lead among you" as appointed servants feel a keen responsibility for each one in the congregation. As stated at Hebrews 13:17, "They are keeping watch over

your souls as those who will render an account."
They endeavor to set a fine example for the
congregation, and they encourage all to take
full advantage of provisions made by the organization for their spiritual welfare. But their position
is not that of bosses, trying to run the lives of
other persons. They are well acquainted with
what Jesus said, as recorded at Mark 10:42-44:
"You know that those who appear to be ruling
the nations lord it over them and their great ones
wield authority over them. This is not the way
among you; but whoever wants to become great
among you must be your minister, and whoever
wants to be first among you must be the slave
of all." In harmony with this, appointed servants
in the congregations of Jehovah's witnesses are
not addressed with any titles designed to elevate
them above others. They are our Christian
brothers.—Job 32:21, 22; Matt. 23:8-11.

As our brothers, they deserve the love of each
one of us. And as appointed servants in Jehovah's
organization, they deserve our deep respect and
cooperation. When writing to the congregation
of the Thessalonians, the apostle Paul admonished: "Now we request you, brothers, to have
regard for those who are working hard among
you and presiding over you in the Lord and
admonishing you; and to give them more than
extraordinary consideration in love because of
their work." (1 Thess. 5:12, 13) That is good
advice for us too. Further, the Bible counsels us
to 'imitate the faith' of these brothers who speak
the word of God to us, 'to be obedient and submissive.' (Heb. 13:7, 17) "Older men who preside
in a fine way" are to be "reckoned worthy of
double honor, especially those who work hard in
speaking and teaching." (1 Tim. 5:17) In this way
we show our devotion to Jehovah, whom they
represent in their positions of oversight, and we

put ourselves in position to benefit to the full from their loving service on our behalf.

APPOINTMENT OF SERVANTS

Those who are overseers in the congregations of Jehovah's witnesses are appointed theocratically. They are not selected on the basis of their success in business affairs of the world but in harmony with the qualifications set out in God's own Word the Bible. Years of faithful service are prized over youthful vigor, and spirituality is valued more than natural ability. Men who qualify to be overseers are described in this way: "The overseer should therefore be irreprehensible, a husband of one wife, moderate in habits, sound in mind, orderly, hospitable, qualified to teach, not a drunken brawler, not a smiter, but reasonable, not belligerent, not a lover of money, a man presiding over his own household in a fine manner, having children in subjection with all seriousness; . . . not a newly converted man . . . Moreover, he should also have a fine testimony from people on the outside." (1 Tim. 3:2-7; see also Titus 1:5-9.) The resident overseer, or presiding minister, of each congregation of Jehovah's witnesses is known as the congregation servant. He is a spiritually mature person to whom you should be able to turn with confidence that the counsel he gives will adhere firmly to God's own faithful Word.

There are also a number of ministerial servants in each congregation and all these are assistants to the overseer or congregation servant. They include the assistant congregation servant, the Bible study servant, the magazine-territory servant, the literature servant, the accounts servant, the *Watchtower* study servant, the Theocratic Ministry School servant and the book study servants. Qualifications to be met by them before being appointed are also listed in the Bible, as follows: "Ministerial servants should likewise be serious, not double-tongued, not giving themselves to a lot of wine, not greedy of dishonest gain, holding the sacred secret of the faith with a clean conscience. Also, let these be tested as to fitness first, then let them serve as ministers, as they are free from accusation. Let ministerial servants be husbands of one wife, presiding in a fine manner over children and their own households. For the men who minister in a fine manner are acquiring for themselves a fine standing and great freeness of speech in the faith in connection with Christ Jesus." (1 Tim. 3:8-10, 12, 13) They, too, are appointed in a theocratic manner.

When the need arises for servants, the local service committee (the congregation servant, the assistant congregation servant and the Bible study servant) meet together to consider the matter prayerfully. (Luke 6:12, 13) It is their responsibility to review the Scriptural qualifications and recommend brothers who fit the Bible's standard. Those recommended should be men who show appreciation for the congregation meetings by regular attendance and participation, are zealous in the field ministry, go out of their way to aid other publishers and are respected in the congregation for their exemplary Christian conduct. Their recommendation is then sent to the Watch Tower Bible and Tract Society of Pennsylvania, the legal agency used by the visible governing body of Jehovah's witnesses.

When submitting a recommendation to the Society, the committee shows the full name of the one being recommended, age, years in service, date of immersion, whether of the anointed or "other sheep," also average hours of field service, back-calls and home Bible studies for the past six months. Additionally, they are requested to include comments on the spirituality of the brother, as reflected in a comparison of him with the Scriptural requirements. When a congregation servant or assistant congregation servant is being recommended, his complete mailing address and phone number (if he has one) are also provided. If the committee is unanimous in recommending the brother, only one name needs to be submitted; however, if more than one qualified person is available, they may submit a first and second recommendation. The Society is not bound by the recommendation submitted, but is pleased to consider it. If it is acceptable, a letter of appointment will be sent to the congregation. This is in harmony with the arrangement in the early Jerusalem congregation, where recommendation of servants was made to the apostles, and then these members of the Christian governing body prayed and conferred authority upon the men who had been certified by the other brothers.—Acts 6:3-6.

Of course, in making recommendations to the Society, certain questions may arise in view of local circumstances. How are these problems resolved? The counsel of God's Word lights the way. True, the brothers available in one locality may not manifest all the desired qualities to the same degree that those in another place do, but the ones who show the greatest spirituality are chosen to serve. If they show themselves willing and constantly seek Jehovah's direction, his spirit makes up for their lack. And, as was done in the first-century congregation, other responsible ones in the theocratic organization offer them assistance and counsel in carrying on their work in a way well pleasing to God.—Acts 20:17, 28; Phil. 1:1; 2 Tim. 1:6.

Nevertheless, the Scriptures are very pointed in saying that no "newly converted man" should be designated as an overseer and that a man should be "tested as to fitness" before he is appointed as a ministerial servant. (1 Tim. 3:6, 10) So, even

where there is a scarcity of brothers, it is required
that a man have a record of a minimum of one
year of exemplary service after his immersion
before he can be considered for assignment as a
servant. But those longer in the truth are pre-
ferred when available. If there are not enough
qualified brothers to care for all the assignments,
those who do qualify may be asked to care for
more than one servant's position, and assistants
can help them to do the work while themselves
receiving training.

If there are still not sufficient brothers to care
for the necessary work, then, on recommendation
from the congregation committee, the Society
may request that certain mature, humble sisters
assist. They are not appointed as servants, but
are simply requested to be substitutes in caring
for the work until a qualified brother is available.
This is in harmony with the fact that, when Jesus
ascended to heaven, he gave "gifts in men" to
provide oversight for the Christian congregation;
also, we are told that overseers are to be spiritually "older men"; and, consistently, those overseers
and ministerial servants who were married are
spoken of as "husbands."—Eph. 4:8; Titus 1:5;
1 Tim. 3:1, 2, 12.

Anyone recommended by the committee for appointment as a servant is to be "free from accusation." (Titus 1:7) Servants are to be "examples to
the flock" of God. (1 Pet. 5:3) If there is some
situation that raises questions, the committee
bears the responsibility to determine whether
what the individual is doing causes him to come
under accusation of immature conduct so that the
congregation as a whole will not have confidence
in him. If so, he should not be recommended.
However, it may be that many years ago a
brother engaged in unchristian conduct and was
disfellowshiped but has now been reinstated. Is
he barred forever from being an appointed ser-

vant? Not necessarily. If he repented and has been reinstated for at least ten years, and now manifests proper Christian humility and a strong appreciation of Jehovah's view of the matter in which he formerly erred, and is now viewed by others as a good example to the flock of God, he might be recommended for some service privilege. Perhaps someone else got involved in wrong conduct that did not result in disfellowshiping but, because of his humble, repentant attitude right from the start, was put on probation. It usually is not necessary to wait many years before such a one can serve, but one recommended as a servant should not be presently on probation and he should have set a fine enough example in Christian living since the wrongdoing that he is now viewed by the congregation, not as an immature person, but as a mature Christian 'example to the flock.'

Of course, the service committee should never recommend anyone to the Society for appointment unless they certify that he qualifies to serve in their congregation. However, even when they do recommend a brother, if he was ever on probation or disfellowshiped, this is mentioned to the Society, along with the reason for the action, length of disfellowshipment or probation, and when it terminated. Thus care can be exercised to safeguard the spiritual welfare of the congregations.

Sometimes it proves necessary to recommend the removal of a servant. It may be that, due to personal circumstances, he requests it. Or, perhaps, though he at one time did measure up to the Scriptural qualifications, that is no longer true. This is lovingly discussed with the one involved before a recommendation is made to the Society, and, if possible, he is aided to correct the situation so that he can continue to serve. But, if a change is recommended, complete and specific reasons are included in the letter to the Society.

When discharging this responsibility of recommending servants, those on the congregation service committee are under obligation to keep in mind the sound counsel written by a member of the first-century governing body to a Christian overseer in Ephesus, namely: "Never lay your hands hastily upon any man; neither be a sharer in the sins of others; preserve yourself chaste." (1 Tim. 5:22) So the members of the committee consider matters carefully, turning to Jehovah in prayer. When they submit recommendations to the Society, all three of them sign it, indicating their agreement on the matter. If there is any uncertainty in their minds on what should be done, they wait for the visit of the circuit servant, discuss it together and then he submits the recommendation to the Society as part of his report on the congregation. In fact, if there is no urgency, these matters are frequently reserved for handling at the time of the circuit servant's visit.

The Bible plainly says that those who occupy positions of oversight in the Christian congregation have been appointed by holy spirit. Said Paul to the older men of the congregation of Ephesus: "Pay attention to yourselves and to all the flock, among which the holy spirit has appointed you overseers, to shepherd the congregation of God." (Acts 20:28) Just as appointment was by holy spirit then, so it is today. God's own Word, which was written under direction of holy spirit, sets the standard. Those who are appointed are persons who themselves are "full of spirit," manifesting the fruits of God's spirit in their lives. (Acts 6:3; Gal. 5:22, 23) Prayer for God's spirit to direct the matter is offered both by those making the recommendation and by those charged with making the appointment. Furthermore, the appointment is made under the direction of the spirit-anointed "faithful and discreet slave" class. When this arrangement of things is adhered to in every way, we can be confident that the appointments made are, indeed, by means of holy spirit, being in full harmony with Jehovah's will.

Recognizing the high standard that is followed in selecting overseers and ministerial servants for the congregations of Jehovah's people, you can have confidence in them. Never despise their counsel or look down on them as individuals, viewing matters from simply a human standpoint. (2 Cor. 10:7-11; 1 Tim. 4:12; Acts 4:13) Learn to take God's view of matters, appreciating the spiritual qualities that he prizes in his servants. In this way you will be able to benefit from the provision that he has kindly made for your blessing.

In time it may be that you, too, if a male, will qualify for appointment as a servant in the congregation. When you were baptized, you said, in effect, to all onlookers: 'I have made an unreserved dedication of myself to Jehovah God. Whatever his will is, I am willing to do it.' In harmony with your dedication, if you are a male, we urge you to take to heart what Paul wrote to Timothy: "If any man is reaching out for an office of overseer, he is desirous of a fine work." (1 Tim. 3:1) There is a great need for qualified men to shoulder responsibility in the theocratic organization, and rich blessings from Jehovah come to those who are willing to accept such service. You can reach out for these service privileges by applying yourself diligently to measure up to the qualifications for a servant and by showing that you are willing to aid others. Then, when privileges of service of any kind are extended to you, show that you have the spirit of that devoted prophet of God who said: "Here I am! Send me." —Isa. 6:8.

Briefly, now, we would like to acquaint you with the servants in the congregation and their work. They are there to help you.

CONGREGATION SERVANT

The congregation servant is the presiding minister, and he has general oversight of the congregation. He is deeply concerned about the welfare of all who are associated with the congregation. (2 Cor. 11:28, 29) Furthermore, he knows that he is to be "an example to the faithful ones in speaking, in conduct, in love, in faith, in chasteness." (1 Tim. 4:12) He is not a person who simply tells others what to do, but he participates in all the activities of the congregation himself.

His duties include making provision for all the meetings of the congregation and seeing to it that they are conducted properly. He arranges for capable brothers to deliver the public talks that you enjoy, and for chairmen to introduce them. When speakers come from other congregations, he sees that provision is made to extend hospitality to them. (3 John 5-8) There is much work for him to do in connection with the service meeting—planning the program for a month in advance, assigning parts to capable brothers and discussing with them how to adapt the material to local needs, arranging for rehearsal of various parts and caring for his own parts of the program. He also works closely with the *Watchtower* study servant, the Theocratic Ministry School servant and the congregation book study servants, to see that the meetings over which they preside are handled in harmony with the arrangements outlined by the Society, so that they result in the greatest good for all the congregation. He is glad to care for this work, but he cannot do it all himself. All in the congregation share by carrying out their assignments and giving good support to the meetings.

As all of Jehovah's witnesses do, he endeavors to share regularly in the field ministry. He takes the lead in this work, coordinating the arrangements for group witnessing and personally working along with other publishers to assist them in whatever way he can. In order to keep in close touch with all the publishers in their ministry, he arranges to visit the various congregation book studies from time to time and to work with the groups there in the field service. When he visits your service group, if there is opportunity for you to work with him, by all means take advantage of it.

As a shepherd of Jehovah's people, the overseer makes a diligent effort to give loving attention to each one of the flock according to the personal needs of that one. (Jer. 23:4) To the extent possible, he welcomes newcomers to the congregation and commends and encourages those who are already active servants of God. He is interested in assisting each one to become a mature Christian. If some are sick or depressed, he pays them a visit to build them up. (Matt. 25:37-40) He bears in mind what the apostle Paul said to the older men of the early Ephesus congregation: "I have exhibited to you in all things that by thus laboring you must assist those who are weak," and he is glad to offer such assistance. (Acts 20:35) If someone becomes irregular or completely inactive as a publisher, or if one frequently misses meetings, the overseer shows concern about that person. He offers whatever help he can to aid the individual to renew his love for God and to become firm in the faith. (Ezek. 34:16) These are things that you, too, can do as you see the need.

In caring for the interests of the congregation, there are also records that must be kept, and the congregation servant has oversight of these. Even though others may care for them, he checks them periodically. All correspondence from the Society having to do with congregation matters is sent to him, either for reading to the congregation or for attention by various ones of the servants. Orders sent to the Society for literature and handbills, as well as remittance and subscription forms and other congregation correspondence, are signed by him. (Of course, individual publishers are free to write to the Society too, when necessary.) The overseer makes provision for certain items, such as appointment letters from the Society and reports left by circuit servants, to be retained in a permanent file. At all times he seeks to work closely with the governing body and its representatives, responding to its direction and encouraging others to do the same, because he knows that this results in Jehovah's blessing on the congregation.—Acts 16:4, 5.

With a view to continued growth of the organization, the overseer may find it beneficial to arrange for the training of willing ones who someday may qualify for appointment as servants. (2 Tim. 2:1, 2) They can learn by observing and by helping the appointed servant to care for records and other work. Particularly in larger congregations some servants may find that they need assistance to care for their assignment of work; so arrangements for someone to work with them can be doubly beneficial. The congregation servant should approve the assignment of any such assistants before they begin to serve.

The congregation overseer is a man who has personal obligations that require attention too. He may be secularly employed, providing for himself and his family, and that often requires considerable time. If he has a family, he is to be "a man presiding over his own household in a fine manner, having children in subjection with all seriousness." (1 Tim. 3:4) He needs to spend time to care for their physical, emotional and spiritual needs. (1 Tim. 5:8) He also needs opportunities for personal study. So he is not able to spend all his time in caring for congregation matters. Yet he has been kind enough to arrange his affairs to extend assistance, as he is able, to you and all the rest of the congregation.

As you become well acquainted with your congregation servant, we believe you will find that, in many respects, he is like that early Christian overseer the apostle Paul, who wrote: "Having a tender affection for you, we were well pleased to impart to you, not only the good news of God, but also our own souls, because you became beloved to us. In harmony with that you well know how, as a father does his children, we kept exhorting each one of you, and consoling and bearing witness to you, to the end that you should go on walking worthily of God."—1 Thess. 2:8, 11, 12.

ASSISTANT CONGREGATION SERVANT

Next to the congregation overseer, the assistant congregation servant is usually the most competent brother in the congregation. Spiritually speaking, he is an older man, one who has a mature interest in the spiritual welfare of the entire congregation. If anything should happen to the overseer, the assistant would step in and take care of the congregation. Also, he takes oversight of the congregation in the absence of the congregation servant.

Regularly the congregation benefits from his ministry. He has a share in the meetings, and, to the extent that his circumstances permit, he takes the lead in the field ministry.

He is also responsible to care for some of the service records of the congregation. Each week he tabulates the field service reports for the entire congregation, marks the totals on a weekly report sheet supplied by the Society and informs the congregation servant of the report to date. At the end of the month he prepares the congregation's service report card and gives it to the overseer so that he can sign and mail it to the Society no later than the fifth of the following month. He also puts a report of the congregation's field ministry for the month on the information board at the Kingdom Hall, doing so as soon as possible after the service report is sent to the Society. Then, once a month he enters on the Publisher's Record cards each publisher's service report, including reports of pioneers in the congregation; and, when he is finished with them, he passes the Bible study reports on to the Bible study servant.

Yet the assistant congregation servant is by no means merely a record keeper. The reports that he handles reflect the devotion of faithful servants of God, and they indicate where there is need for the appointed servants and other mature ones in the congregation to be of loving assistance to their brothers and sisters. So, about the first of each month when he is making entries on the Publisher's Record cards, he takes note of any who need help in presenting the Kingdom message. Some publishers may be spending time in the service but not placing any literature or not having any results in following up interest shown. From time to time he gives a note on the needs of various ones to the congregation book study servants so that help can be offered, thus producing increased praise to Jehovah and enabling the individual publisher to find greater joy in his service.

If he observes that some did not report any service at all for the month, this information is conveyed to the book study servants right away so that a personal call can be made to offer assistance. He believes that any who have been reporting as Kingdom publishers really do want to serve Jehovah, and he feels a strong obligation to aid them to do this regularly. Sometimes a person who is experiencing ill health, opposition from unbelieving family members or other personal problems gets depressed and deeply appreciates the loving concern of Christian brothers. (1 Thess. 5:11, 14) With a little help, such a one may be glad to get out in the field service again. On the other hand, if any who are not reporting have not been attending the congregation meetings either and so have lost their desire to participate in the service, what they need is personal help to be strengthened spiritually in order to stay on the road to life. (Matt. 7:13, 14) Perhaps arrangements can be made to help them get back into the habit of regular meeting attendance. It may even be that some need a home Bible study to be conducted with them again. The servants are glad to be of help. They feel about them as does Jehovah, of whom his Son said: "It is not a desirable thing with my Father who is in heaven for one of these little ones to perish."—Matt. 18: 12-14.

At the fifteenth of each month, too, the assistant congregation servant notifies the book study servants of any who have not yet reported service for the month. We feel sure that any who are publishers want to be regular in their service, reporting every month if at all possible. But some may need help; others may simply have forgotten to turn in their report slip. Obviously, you can help to keep the assistant congregation servant's work in this regard at a minimum by remembering to turn in your service reports regularly each week.

If a new publisher reports field service for the first time, this makes us rejoice. But, before the report is counted, it is wise to make sure that the individual qualifies to be a publisher and that he appreciates what it means to be publicly identified as an associate of Jehovah's witnesses, in training for the ministry. So the assistant congregation servant notifies the overseer, and then the overseer has a personal talk with the individual, highlighting the righteous requirements of Jehovah for his people as well as the provisions that God has made to keep us spiritually strong, and warmly commending the new publisher for the progress that he is making. Then the assistant congregation servant makes out a record card for this new publisher and includes it in the file of active publishers in the congregation.

In view of his duties, we feel sure that you can see why this brother is called the assistant congregation servant. He works closely with the overseer and endeavors to be a real assistant. However, this service is performed on behalf of you and your brothers and sisters in the congregation. Understanding what is done, you can benefit from it and can work along with this servant in aiding others to be regular praisers of our God.

BIBLE STUDY SERVANT

Although the Bible study servant shares in all features of the service, he is particularly interested in promoting back-call and Bible study activity on the part of all the publishers in the congregation. He is a mature brother, one who has had considerable experience in the ministry, and he will gladly assist you in this activity.

When any back-call slips are received from the Society, he distributes them to the various book study servants so that they will be given attention. If you are handed such a slip by your book study servant, be sure to make the call promptly. Perhaps repeated calls will be needed in order to make contact, but it is good to persevere. These are individuals who have shown some interest in the truth, but they are in need of further attention. The same is true of those on your own back-call list, persons whose names you noted on your house-to-house record because they listened appreciatively to your sermon or accepted some literature. Their lives are involved; give them every opportunity to accept the truth. If you need someone to go along with you on the call, or simply suggestions on how to deal with a particular situation, remember, your Bible study servant will be glad to help.

If possible, the Bible study servant would like to see every publisher in the congregation conducting at least one home Bible study. He knows that this is one of the most important means by which the sheeplike ones are being gathered into Jehovah's organization. He appreciates, too, the joy that conducting a study can bring to the publisher. Are you presently conducting a study? If so, you are well aware that it is largely from this activity that new praisers of Jehovah come, and you know the contentment that sharing in such work brings. If you do not have a study, the Bible study servant may approach you to offer some aid. On the other hand, if you really want to conduct a study but are having some difficulty in getting one started, why not take the initiative by talking to the Bible study servant about it?

To afford opportunity for this brother to work with the publishers long enough to get them well established in the back-call and Bible study work, he usually spends considerable time with the group that meets at a service rendezvous. He may even be assigned as the congregation book study servant there, so that he can concentrate on the work in that locality. Then, when he has accomplished what appears to be possible, he may be assigned by the congregation servant to another congregation book study for a period of time— perhaps a few months, or even a year or more.

The Bible study servant keeps a record of all the Bible studies being conducted in the congregation's territory. In his file he has a separate Study Record slip for each study, whether it is conducted by a congregation publisher or a pioneer. All of them are arranged alphabetically according to the names of the householders. As soon as you report a new home Bible study, he makes out a Study Report slip and includes it in the file. Then, each month when you turn in your Study Report slip, he makes the necessary entries to keep it up-to-date. Of course, not all studies continue; and if you find that there is no further interest, do not forget to mark your Study Report slip "not interested" so that the corresponding record can be removed from the file. There is also a section in his file where he keeps study records for each of the congregation meetings, and from the Study Report slips submitted at the end of the month by the ones in charge of the various meetings, he records the number of meetings held and the average attendance. The Study Report slips, having served their purpose, are then destroyed. But the file itself is a guide to the Bible study servant in offering assistance to both publishers and newly interested ones.

If you are conducting a home Bible study, from time to time the Bible study servant may inquire about it. In fact, if you approach him and tell him what progress is being made, he appreciates it. He is keenly interested in the advancement being made by all of these potential servants of God. If any problems arise in connection with the study, he is pleased to offer suggestions. And, where possible, he likes to get acquainted with these persons, and thus help you to get them in closer touch with the congregation.

Should circumstances arise that make it impossible for you to care for a certain study anymore, feel free to seek the Bible study servant's help in arranging for someone else to conduct it. Or, if you are getting good results in this feature of the service, and would be willing to take someone else along with you and help him to start a study, tell the Bible study servant that you would like to help. There is much of this work to be done, and willing workers are needed.

CONGREGATION COMMITTEE

The congregation servant, the assistant congregation servant and the Bible study servant comprise what is known as the congregation committee. While the congregation servant is the one who is responsible to take full oversight of the congregation, there are times when it is beneficial for several mature brothers to discuss matters together. (Prov. 15:22) The congregation servant acts as the chairman of this group.

Certain recommendations are submitted to the Society, for example, and these are given attention by the entire committee. When the need arises, they prayerfully consider together which brothers are Scripturally qualified for appointment by the Society as servants. Similarly, applications for regular pioneer service and for appointment as vacation pioneers are checked by the committee and, if approved, are submitted to the Society. If it is deemed advisable to divide a congregation into two units, this too is weighed by the committee before being sent to the Society for approval. Such recommendations to the Society are signed by all three members of the committee.

Public speakers in the congregations are not appointed by the Society, but they too care for a very responsible assignment, so their selection is a matter that is handled by the committee.

Other matters may be discussed by the committee and then submitted, not to the Society, but to the local congregation. Changing meeting times to make them convenient to the majority of the publishers is one of these. Arrangements for an adequate place of meeting is another. Whether it is a matter of finding a better hall to rent or purchasing property and building a Kingdom Hall, the congregation as a whole bears the expense; so the matter is put to them for decision. The same is true of sending contributions of money to the Society to be used to advance the Kingdom interests, and setting aside funds for legal cases that may involve the preaching work locally. In many places the State makes provision for needy persons, but there may be situations involving worthy individuals that require loving consideration by the congregation, and, of course, it is up to the congregation to decide what they are in position to do. (1 Tim. 5:3-16; Rom. 12:13) After the committee has come to agreement on any of these matters having to do with the congregation, it is presented to the congregation for decision. Particularly if it involves the use of congregation funds the committee's recommendation is drawn up in the form of a written resolution. The congregation servant presents the resolution to the congregation, and the congregation is free to discuss the matter from all angles before it is voted on. Then, if the congregation accepts the resolution after hearing all the facts and votes in approval of it, the committee will follow through in caring for what has been approved.

The committee may, at times, call in other mature publishers for advice when they are discussing certain matters. However, the committee is responsible to draw its own conclusions and write up the resolution or recommendation to present either to the congregation or to the Society, depending on the matter under consideration.

At times the committee is called on to act in a judicial capacity in handling difficulties that arise and in keeping the congregation clean and acceptable to Jehovah. (1 Cor. 5:12–6:6) Usually this judicial committee is made up of the same three brothers who comprise the service committee discussed above. But, if there are not three qualified brothers available locally, or if one of the committee asks to be permitted to step aside for some reason, a qualified brother from another congregation may be requested to serve by the other two members. Wherever possible, these brothers seek to assist persons who sincerely want to serve Jehovah acceptably, but they are also well aware of the obligation not to ignore Jehovah's righteous judicial decisions. (Gal. 6:1; Ps. 119: 106) They encourage the congregation always to be guided by the wise counsel in God's own Word, and they endeavor to do the same themselves.

MAGAZINE-TERRITORY SERVANT

The magazine-territory servant has been given the assignment of supplying you with copies of the *Watchtower* and *Awake!* magazines to use in the field service and territory in which to work. He is pleased when he can serve you.

Each congregation usually has a day set aside in which magazine distribution is particularly featured, and it is the magazine-territory servant's assignment to give this his special attention. He takes particular interest in seeing to it that there are convenient arrangements for publishers to meet for this activity, and he works closely with the congregation servant to accomplish it. It may be that he has approached you and asked if you would like to work with one of the Magazine Day service groups. If you can arrange to do so, we know that you will enjoy it. But if that particular day is not convenient for you, choose a time that fits your schedule, and share regularly in this feature of Kingdom service.

In order to have magazines with which to work, you will need to place an order with the magazine-territory servant. This should be a regular standing order. He will add your requirements to the number already being received and, if necessary, notify the congregation servant of the increase.

Such adjustments in the order, as well as requests for an extra supply of a particular issue, are sent to the Society on the magazine Distributors' Order blank. For orders of thirty or more, the brothers endeavor to order in tens, because it helps the Society in its mailing; so there may be a few extra copies available at the counter if you place your supply of a certain issue faster than usual. But if you find that you can make good use of even more copies of any issue, do not hesitate to ask for them. The brothers are pleased to order them, and the Society will send them out just as quickly as possible. Whatever you order, be sure to take them. The congregation has obtained them from the Society for you on credit, and the magazine-territory servant depends on each one to take his supply so that the account does not become delinquent.

When the magazines are received from the Society, the magazine-territory servant counts them, checks the total against the label on the package and informs the accounts servant of the issue and the number of magazines received. If there is a discrepancy, the congregation servant notifies the Society, so that the account can be adjusted. They are then made available to you at the first meeting after they arrive, and you will find that the magazine-territory servant is usually at the Kingdom Hall for at least twenty minutes before and after meetings to serve you. Please pay for the magazines when you receive them. This money (with a notation of the total placed with pioneers) is turned over to the accounts servant each week. Obviously, if his records are going to balance, it is important that no one help himself to magazines when the servant in charge is not there.

The magazine-territory servant also has charge of the file of territory in which those associated with the congregation carry out their field service. Congregation publishers, pioneers and congregation book study servants all get their assignments of territory through the magazine-territory servant. As long as a territory is available in the file, they may take their choice of where they would like to work. But only as much territory as is actually needed for the present is to be checked out at any one time. If you hold a personal territory, do not forget that as soon as it has been worked once, or at the end of four months, even if it has not been completed, it should be checked in. If you are caring for it and want to check it out again, you may do that, but the servant in charge needs your help if he is going to keep an accurate record of the work being done.

The congregation's entire assignment of territory is subdivided into small sections, each containing perhaps 200 to 300 homes and each bearing its own number. However, the type of territory and local circumstances influence the size. This breakdown of the territory is also generally shown on a map of the entire area, with boundaries and territory numbers clearly marked. This makes it easy to select the section in which you would like to work.

When you request territory in which to work, the magazine-territory servant may make a suggestion concerning sections that are particularly in need of attention. Of course, you are free to select the one that you want, but he knows which areas are most in need of attention and endeavors to arrange for a balanced coverage of the congregation's entire assignment with Bible sermons and the campaign offers as well as magazine distribution. If some territories are not regularly worked by individual publishers, he may encourage book study servants to care for them in group witnessing and they may be given attention by groups on Magazine Day. It is hoped that all the territory can be covered every four months, and more often if possible.

If the congregation's assignment of territory contains a large rural area or a number of towns spread out over a large area, the public meetings are sometimes scheduled in these localities away from the Kingdom Hall in order to concentrate work in sections that are not regularly given attention. The distribution of handbills in connection with these meetings, whether held at the Kingdom Hall or elsewhere, keeps the Kingdom work before the public. The magazine-territory servant has charge of the handbill supply, and he endeavors to see that all of them are used. If the time for their use is running out and there are still some on hand, he may suggest that some of the publishers simply work through a section of territory putting them under the doors of the homes. This is something that even young ones can do and enjoy.

Other means of advertising the Kingdom message also come within the assignment of the magazine-territory servant. For example, if you have a window display at the Kingdom Hall, he usually is the one who cares for it. And if you find a notice in a local newspaper concerning the congregation meetings, or perhaps concerning the visit of the circuit servant or travel by the publishers to an assembly, he probably had a hand in it.

He always discusses these matters with the congregation servant before starting anything new, but then he follows through on the details of the work. His great interest is to keep the Kingdom message prominently before everyone who lives in the congregation's territory; and, of course, in that work you have a share.

LITERATURE SERVANT

There is a servant in the congregation whose special assignment is to make available to you and the other publishers and pioneers books, booklets, Bibles and tracts for use in the field ministry. He is the literature servant.

Regularly he checks the congregation's supply of literature and *Kingdom Ministry* announcements of coming literature offers, to be sure that there will be ample literature on hand. Using his records from years past as a guide, he can estimate how much of certain items to order, so that there will be sufficient but not an excess. If there is some item of literature that you would like to have, perhaps in a foreign language that he does not have in stock, he will be glad to include it in his next order to the Society. In most congregations an order is sent just once a month, after the close of the month. For your convenience, the literature servant plans to have the literature room open for about twenty minutes before and after meetings at the Kingdom Hall. But no one should ever help himself to literature when the servant in charge is not there.

Most of the literature in stock belongs to the Society, having been obtained by the congregation on credit. So the literature servant realizes that there is a responsibility on his part to take good care of it, keeping it neat and clean, and to keep accurate records. Whenever you obtain literature from him, he carefully marks on a Literature Check Sheet the amount taken. Then at least once a week he totals everything moved from the stock and gives a copy of the Literature Check Sheet to the accounts servant along with the corresponding money. If it is necessary, on occasion, to place small amounts of literature with a publisher on credit, he makes notation of it on a Publisher's Credit Slip and asks the publisher to sign it. But no further credit is extended until the literature previously obtained has been paid for. Then, when payment is made, the literature servant shows the movement of the literature on his Literature Check Sheet for the week.

Pioneers, too, obtain their literature supplies from the congregation, paying for it at pioneer rates. Since the pioneers receive their literature at less than cost, to help them with expenses, separate records are kept at the literature room. What they obtain is recorded on a separate Literature Check Sheet, and at the end of the month credit is requested from the Society for the difference in rates.

When a shipment of literature is received from the Society, the literature servant opens it soon and checks it against the invoice to be sure that everything is in order. After he marks it approved or notes any needed correction he passes it on to the congregation servant, who checks it and turns it over to the accounts servant for filing. If there are any discrepancies, the overseer writes to the Society about it right away.

Whatever supplies come from the Society are noted on the Progressive Inventory kept by the literature servant, and at the end of the month he enters the total amount of each publication moved from the stock. This enables him to figure just what he has on hand. He keeps such an inventory for each language in which he has a supply of literature. Additionally, each year, on September 1, he makes an actual-count inventory and sends a report of the results to the Society on a form provided at that time. So, as you can see, the servants endeavor to handle these matters in a very orderly way, as befits Jehovah's people.

ACCOUNTS SERVANT

The accounts servant is charged with the responsibility of caring for money that you and others contribute locally for the advancement of the Kingdom work, as well as any other funds handled by the congregation. He keeps a careful record of all money received and disbursed, and any expenditures of money are approved by the congregation overseer. The method of accounting used is outlined in detail in instructions provided by the Society to each congregation.

No collection is ever taken at the meetings of Jehovah's people, nor is there any assessment of dues. Expenses of the congregation are met by voluntary contributions. (1 Chron. 29:1, 2, 5, 9) For your convenience, contribution boxes are provided by the accounts servant at the Kingdom Hall and at all the locations where congregation book studies are held.—2 Ki. 12:9, 10.

The accounts servant has many details for which to care. A number of things require his attention after each meeting; others are cared for once a week. For example, after each meeting contributions are taken from the box and the amount is noted on a Receipt form. A duplicate copy of the Receipt goes to the congregation servant, and the accounts servant enters the amount on the Account Sheet. At least once a week money is also received from the literature and magazine-territory servants, Receipts are made out for them, a copy of each is retained by the accounts servant and appropriate entries are made on the Account Sheet.

When you obtain a magazine subscription, or want to renew your own, be sure that you have made it out neatly and accurately, then give it to the accounts servant and he will see that it gets prompt attention. He makes out a Receipt for the total amount of subscription money received at any one meeting, keeps the Receipt in his file and makes an entry on the Account Sheet. Then, once a week, he fills out a Subscription Record Sheet, listing all the subscriptions received that week, and gives it to the overseer, with the subscription slips and covering Remittance and Credit Request form and corresponding remittance, to be checked and sent to the Society. A copy of the Subscription Record Sheet is retained in the accounts servant's file.

Some matters require attention once a month. For example, by the fifth of each month a remittance is made to the Society of all money received from the literature and magazine-territory servants during the preceding month, and credit is requested for items placed with pioneers. A Remittance and Credit Request form signed by the congregation servant is used for this purpose. Also, the accounts servant balances the records for the month and prepares a financial report to read to the congregation.

To assure the accuracy of the accounts, as well as for the protection of both the congregation and the accounts servant, the overseer arranges to have the accounts audited every three months—at the beginning of March, June, September and December. All invoices, carbon copies of Remittance and Credit Request forms, and magazine labels are kept in a "pending" file until such time as they appear on the Society's statements; then they are transferred to a permanent file. Magazine labels and Literature Check Sheets are retained only until the audit is made. However, Accounts Sheets, Receipts, Invoices, Credit Memos, Statements, Remittance and Credit Request forms, Subscription Record Sheets, bills, bank statements, check stubs and canceled checks are retained in the permanent file for a period of seven years or whatever the Statute of Limitations requires in your locality.

Some congregations find it convenient to have a bank account in which to deposit their funds each week, and that is all right if they want to do it. Where it is done, the account is in the name of the " . . . . . Congregation of Jehovah's Witnesses." If there is more than one congregation in the city, then the name is " . . . . . Congregation of Jehovah's Witnesses, ... Unit." All checks drawn on the account are signed by the accounts servant and countersigned by the congregation servant. Other congregations may prefer to use money orders, bank drafts or other safe method of transmitting money. Nevertheless, the expenditures are always approved by the overseer.

This care given to the handling of funds of the congregation assures that they will all be used in the way intended, to advance the Kingdom interests.

"WATCHTOWER" STUDY SERVANT

The *Watchtower* study servant leads the congregation in its weekly study of the *Watchtower* magazine, which is the principal publication of "the faithful and discreet slave" class. (Matt. 24: 45-47) He has the assignment of helping everyone in the congregation to get full benefit from this spiritual provision that Jehovah has made for his people.

Realizing that, he endeavors to set aside time to make a special study of each lesson. Where possible, he may go over the material carefully several times to get it clearly in mind. Furthermore, he endeavors to get a clear view of the overall objective of the article and the principal points developed, so that he can aid the congregation to see these. Having such a grasp of the material enables him to know where repetition for emphasis in the study will be helpful, which points bear specially careful discussion because they are key ideas, and which ones are relatively minor in relation to the discussion at hand. His is more than a routine assignment of asking questions. He wants to help everyone present to understand the material thoroughly and appreciate its application to their lives as Christian witnesses of Jehovah. —Prov. 4:7.

He has a personal interest in the spiritual growth of all in the congregation, and he knows that regularly being at the *Watchtower* study is a major factor in one's advancement to Christian maturity. So, if some are not attending regularly, he tries to visit them personally; and he works through the congregation book study servants to encourage them to be present each week, to the extent possible.

Also, he would like to see those who are in attendance benefit from the study most fully. He knows that the ones who are active participants get more from the meeting and enjoy it much more than do passive listeners. So, as opportunity affords, he talks to those who need help along this line and offers to assist them to prepare an answer or discusses with them how to pick out and underscore key thoughts and use them in commenting. If you realize that you are not actively participating in the study each week and want some aid, why not approach your *Watchtower* study servant and discuss the matter with him? He will count it a privilege to help you. —Heb. 10:23-25.

On the other hand, if you are an active participant in the meeting, there is much that you can do to aid others to do the same. What about the members of your family, those with whom you conduct studies and who are now attending the Kingdom Hall meetings, also the publishers with whom you closely associate in the field service? Do they all attend regularly and comment freely? Would you like to help them? Why not select just one who needs some encouragement and patiently offer it? When you see good results, we are sure that you will be moved to aid others too. In this way you can cooperate with the *Watchtower* study servant in helping your brothers to get the full benefit from the rich spiritual provisions that Jehovah is now making through his organization.

THEOCRATIC MINISTRY SCHOOL SERVANT

The brother who presides over the Theocratic Ministry School is the Theocratic Ministry School servant. Among the brothers in the congregation, he is usually one who has a particularly good knowledge of both Bible truth and the language of the country and is able to express himself well. He is keenly interested in improvement of the speaking and teaching ability of everyone in the congregation.

The outline of material to be covered in the Theocratic Ministry School is provided by the Society, and the school servant follows this in assigning talks to those enrolled. When you are assigned a talk, he usually makes it a point to notify you at least three weeks in advance, so that there is ample time for you to prepare.

If the congregation with which you are associated has a very large enrollment in the school, you may find that it is divided into two or more sections for the student talks. In this way each one has an opportunity to give a talk at least every three months. The congregation servant arranges for capable assistants to the school servant to offer counsel to the students in the additional groups.

For the school servant (and any assistants he may have) to give good counsel, it is necessary for them to do considerable preparation each week. They need to be familiar with the material on which each student is going to speak as well as the speech qualities on which each is working. When offering counsel, they always draw attention to good qualities, for the encouragement of the student. And with a view to the student's advancement, they may discuss how he can improve in others and assign him specific speech qualities to give attention to in his next talk. During the meeting they have just two minutes in which to offer counsel to each student speaker, and they try to make what they say in that time beneficial both to the speaker and to the rest of the congregation. After the school, when necessary, they talk to the students privately to elaborate on points that may need further discussion. Always they endeavor to make their suggestions with genuine kindness and Christian love, so you should find their help to be truly upbuilding.—1 Cor. 14:12.

Even the school servant may give student talks on occasion, as well as instruction talks. When he does that, the congregation servant or someone else that he may designate offers counsel. So, you see, all of us can continue to learn, and we should all desire to develop as fully as possible our capabilities as servants of God.

As we have learned to be true of the other servants, so with the school servant, he is interested in being of assistance to you, not only from the platform, but personally. If you find that you need help in preparing a talk, in selecting a practical setting for it, or in mastering a particular speech quality, do not hesitate to approach him. He is an experienced and mature brother and he will be able to offer helpful suggestions.

For your use, the congregation also provides at the Kingdom Hall a Theocratic Ministry School library. It is under the supervision of the school servant, and usually it contains all the available publications of the Society, perhaps a variety of Bible translations, an exhaustive concordance and some other helpful reference works. Feel free to use any of these publications at the Kingdom Hall before or after meetings. If you want to take one home with you for a few days, check with the school servant first and he will, no doubt, be glad to accommodate you. The library has been provided for your benefit.

CONGREGATION BOOK STUDY SERVANTS

A key role in the spiritual growth of each congregation is played by the congregation book study servants. Their duties are threefold: to conduct the congregation book studies, to take the lead in the field ministry, and to give the needed personal attention to each one so that all enjoy good spiritual health. Since each book study servant is assigned to give attention to a comparatively small group of publishers, they are able to keep in close touch with each one of the Lord's "sheep" entrusted to their care.

As is true of other servants, each congregation book study servant is appointed by the Society. Then he is assigned to a specific book study group by the congregation servant and is given the names and addresses of all the publishers associated with it. The number of book study servants in the congregation is the same as the number of congregation book studies presently in operation. Then, when definite arrangements are made for a new study group, recommendation is made to the Society of a qualified brother to care for it. In the meantime, prospective servants are appointed by the overseer to serve as assistants to the book study servants, both for training and to care for the study and service arrangements when the appointed servant is not able to be there. If at all possible, each book study servant has an assistant.

To do a really good job of conducting the study each week, the book study servant usually has to spend more time in preparation for the meeting than other publishers do. He needs to know, not only the answers to the study questions, but the reasons for those answers and the value of the information. At the study itself, since the group is moderate in size, he is able to give more personal attention to each one who attends. It is his desire, not merely to cover material, but to aid each one to understand it clearly so that it will be readily available for use in making personal decisions and in teaching others. He knows that a truly informative study, well supported, is a major factor in spiritual growth and a stimulus to participation in the field service.

The location where the book study is held is also a rendezvous from which field service is carried on, and the book study servant takes the lead in this. From time to time he endeavors to go along personally in the service with each one in the group, aiding the less experienced and encouraging those who do well. He knows that regularity in the ministry is important, so he encourages all to have some share in the service each week, if possible. He arranges meetings for group witnessing at times convenient to the circumstances of the publishers, and he is with them himself as often as he can be. When he is not able to be with them, he sees to it that an assistant cares for the group and has territory in which they can work. If there are any who are new in the service, or who can be helped to become better teachers, he also sees that arrangements are made to provide them with a qualified companion in service who can offer helpful suggestions.

A truly mature book study servant is, above all, a loving shepherd. He shows a warm personal interest in the spiritual well-being of each one in his study group. He keeps an eye out for them at the Kingdom Hall meetings, expresses appreciation for their share in the *Watchtower* study and aids those who need help with assignments for the Theocratic Ministry School. He does not feel that his responsibility toward them ends when they turn in a field service report for the month. Are they having a share in the service regularly each week? Do they participate in all attainable features of the service? Can they be encouraged to reach out for additional privileges of service?

These are questions that he has in mind as he thinks of the spiritual health of each of the "sheep."

As a shepherd, he likes to keep in close touch with each one of the "flock." From time to time your book study servant may pay you a visit at your home. He feels as did the apostle Paul, who wrote to fellow believers: "I am longing to see you, that I may impart some spiritual gift to you in order for you to be made firm; or, rather, that there may be an interchange of encouragement among you, by each one through the other's faith, both yours and mine."—Rom. 1:11, 12.

Among those of our first-century brothers who showed particular concern for their fellow Christians was Stephanas, and of him and his household we read: "They set themselves to minister to the holy ones . . . they have refreshed my spirit and yours." They were interested in helping their brothers, the same as your book study servant is. The Scriptures urge us to respond to the help of such persons, saying: "May you also keep submitting yourselves to persons of that kind and to everyone co-operating and laboring."—1 Cor. 16:15-18.

Perhaps some in the book study group have become irregular in attending meetings and have not been out in the service of late. Periodically the book study servant receives a note from the assistant congregation servant reminding him of those in need of help. The book study servant is deeply concerned about them, because he does not want to see any drift away from the flock of God because of negligence on his part. (John 17:12) He makes a personal call on them, not to check up on them, but because he cares for them. It may be that they have been ill and are in need of help. Or perhaps personal problems have left them despondent. He endeavors to build them up with a discussion of spiritual matters and offers what assistance appears to be needed to renew their regular association and service with Jehovah's people.

Of course, the book study servants have other responsibilities that require their time and attention too. Usually they are brothers who are secularly employed, and there are always personal affairs that press for attention. As with the other appointed ministerial servants in the congregation, if they have a family, they are to preside "in a fine manner over children and their own households." (1 Tim. 3:12) That means that they need to spend time with their family. Yet their devotion to Jehovah and their loving concern for others in the congregation move them to expend themselves willingly on behalf of these too. We can surely say of these servants, as an apostle of Jesus Christ said of his Christian brother Epaphroditus: "Keep holding men of that sort dear." —Phil. 2:25, 29.

PUBLIC SPEAKERS

In each congregation, it is up to the congregation committee to determine which ones of the brothers should be used as public speakers. While speaking ability is important, more is required. There are a number of factors that are considered. Is the person dedicated and baptized? Does he have an accurate knowledge of Bible truth? Is he a good teacher, able to express God's Word clearly? When he speaks, does he really hold the interest of his audience? Is he a regular publisher, zealous in the field ministry? regular in attending meetings? a fine example in Christian living? And is he spiritually mature? In the case of one being assigned to give public talks, the answer to each of these questions ought to be Yes.

Only the very best speakers are listed for giving public talks in congregations other than their own. However, there may also be others who are spiritually qualified and who do fairly well as speakers.

Locally the brothers may enjoy hearing them; so arrangements may be made for them to give talks in their own congregation, even though they are not at present being sent out to serve other congregations. While the committee decides who qualify to give public talks, the congregation servant is the one who assigns the specific talks to be prepared by the individual speakers.

In order to have a variety of talks, it is often necessary to obtain speakers from nearby congregations. Such arrangements are always to be approved by the overseer of the speaker's home congregation. After that approval has been obtained, a personal letter is sent to the speaker himself, confirming the subject on which he is to talk, providing the address of the meeting place and the time of the public meeting, along with information concerning arrangements for field service that day.

Normally, those who are appointed servants in a congregation are assigned to give public talks in other congregations only once a month, so that these assignments do not unnecessarily interfere with their caring for responsibilities in their home congregation. However, in some places, to keep the public talks going on a regular basis in the congregations it is necessary for some speakers to be away to give public talks more than once a month. That is all right, provided that the speaker himself is willing to take on the additional responsibility and it will not unduly interfere with his caring for his specific assignment of service in his home congregation. If a brother is assigned to give a talk in a congregation that is a considerable distance away, he may travel there ahead of time and arrange to share with the brothers there in the service during the day. However, if the congregation is close by, either in the same city or nearby, the speaker may prefer to work with his home congregation that day, going to the other congregation only for the meetings.

When a speaker travels a considerable distance, arriving the day before the talk is to be given, it is the privilege of the brothers in the congregation to extend to him Christian hospitality. Even if he arrives on the day of the talk, it is a kind thing to invite him to share a meal. (Rom. 12:13) The congregation servant usually makes arrangements for this, but if you let him know that you will be glad to help out, you may have the opportunity to enjoy the upbuilding association of some of these mature brothers in your own home.

CHAPTER 7

Forming New Congregations

A S THE preaching of the good news is accomplished and sheeplike ones are gathered into Jehovah's organization, the number of congregations also increases. (Acts 14:21-23) Sometimes a group of dedicated and baptized publishers who have been carrying on their ministry in a locality isolated from other congregations is organized into a congregation. Or it may be that a congregation already in operation has grown large, or that the size of the Kingdom Hall or the distance that some travel to the meetings makes it advisable to form a new congregation.

In any event, if a congregation is to be formed, it must be made up of a group of ministers, dedicated and baptized servants of Jehovah God who really love him and want to advance the interests of true worship. There should also be available enough qualified persons to care for the work of the appointed servants. It is not good to be hasty, only to have a congregation that is too weak to function properly. Those who make up the group ought to appreciate that there are responsibilities as well as privileges attached to their being organized into a congregation.

The matter should be thoroughly discussed by those involved, whether an isolated group of publishers, or the congregation committee in the case of division of an already-existing congregation. Then, before the application for formation of the congregation is filed with the Society, it is usually advisable to discuss the matter with the circuit servant.

In naming our congregations we follow the Biblical precedent, designating each congregation by the name of the city or town in which it is located. (1 Cor. 1:2; 1 Thess. 1:1) If more than one congregation functions within a city, then a geographic designation describing its location is added as a unit name. For example: New York, New York, Congregation, Brooklyn Heights Unit; or Saginaw, Michigan, East Unit.

The Society deals with each unit as a separate congregation, sending supplies directly to it and receiving its monthly service report. However, one of the congregation servants is also appointed by the Society as city servant. He does not exercise any jurisdiction over any unit other than his own. However, the Society may wish to communicate with him at times in connection with arrangements for assemblies and other matters. He may also be called on by the overseers of the other units for counsel if some special need arises.

SMALL CONGREGATIONS AND ISOLATED PUBLISHERS

Small congregations, whether newly formed or longer in operation, endeavor to arrange the same program of theocratic activity as larger ones. Material is provided for them to use as the basis for their congregation meetings, and they have the same responsibility as to public proclamation of the "everlasting good news" as their brothers elsewhere do.—Rev. 14:6.

Even if there are only a few in attendance at the congregation meetings, there can be an interchange of encouragement. Discussion of the study material provided by the Society will be upbuilding. Furthermore, as Jesus Christ said: "Where there are two or three gathered together in my name, there I am in their midst." (Matt. 18:20) So, the meetings are no less important just because the attendance may be comparatively small.

Regardless of the size of the congregation, the regular study procedure can be followed at the *Watchtower* study and the congregation book study. If there are not enough persons to prepare all the various service meeting parts, at least they can read and discuss the material together. Similarly, adjustments can be made in the Theocratic Ministry School. If possible, it is good to arrange for the instruction talk to be given as a model talk each week and to have at least one student talk on which counsel is given. But, if necessary, the other assignments can be covered by somewhat informal reports, discussions between two sisters, questions and answers or simply reading the published information. For public meetings, local brothers can no doubt give talks from time to time; occasionally, arrangements can probably be made for visiting speakers, and this will be a stimulus to the group. And, when no speaker is available, the group can even read together one of the extensive outlines provided by the Society and look up the scriptures together. Thus, all congregations, regardless of size, can benefit to the full from the spiritual "food at the proper time" that is being provided through the "faithful and discreet slave."—Matt. 24:45.

If a congregation is composed entirely of sisters, various ones who are spiritually mature and humble will be designated as substitutes to care for the work of the appointed servants until such time as qualified brothers are available. Of course, in recognition of the theocratic arrangement of things, sisters who pray or preside at congregation meetings, because of the absence of a qualified male, wear a head covering. (1 Cor. 11:3-16) With head properly covered, the sisters designated by the Society preside at the various meetings—in most cases, simply seated facing the group. None of the sisters give actual discourses at their meetings, but they read and comment on the material provided by the Society, doing so from their seats. For variety, they may also cover some things by discussions between two of them or in demonstrations. When counseling other sisters in the Theocratic Ministry School, the one conducting that meeting usually just reads excerpts from the Society's publications, thus letting the publications do the teaching. But if a male enrolls in the school, she leaves the counseling of him to the circuit servant. When a *qualified* male becomes available in the congregation, the circuit servant notifies the Society, and that brother is appointed as congregation servant, *Watchtower* study servant, Theocratic Ministry School servant and congregation book study servant. However, until such time as there are other qualified brothers there, the sisters may continue to assist by caring for work normally done by the other appointed servants. This makes it possible for those associated with the congregation to have all their various needs in connection with the ministry given adequate attention.

When the Society is advised of a publisher or a group of publishers living in territory not assigned to any congregation, provision is made to care for their spiritual needs too. If possible, that territory will be assigned to a nearby congregation so that they will be given attention as part of a congregation of Jehovah's people. If the congregations are too far away, they can still arrange to have some or all of the regular congregation meetings, and the Society will supply them with literature and receive reports from them just as it does from the congregations everywhere. In time, perhaps a congregation can be organized. No matter where we may be on earth, we need to keep in close touch with Jehovah's organization and active in the work of disciple-making. The Lord is with us when we do his will, so we should press on in the work with full confidence in him.—2 Tim. 4:7.

CHAPTER 8

Traveling Overseers

TO STIMULATE the spiritual growth of all the congregations of Jehovah's servants, provision is made by the Society for periodic visits by traveling overseers. Some of these visit congregations; others visit circuits, and yet others serve the Society's branch offices and missionary homes. This arrangement affords a fine opportunity for even those who are overseers to receive counsel and encouragement and to discuss any problems with mature representatives of the Society. You, too, benefit from the visits of these traveling overseers. For example, consider how this is true of the visit of the

CIRCUIT SERVANT

To assist all congregations, large and small, as well as isolated publishers, the Society arranges for regular visits by circuit servants, who are appointed by the Society. These spiritually "older men" view matters as did the apostle Paul, who, after having worked with the brothers in quite a number of places, said: "Above all things, let us return and visit the brothers in every one of the cities in which we published the word of Jehovah to see how they are." And he did just that, "strengthening the congregations" as he served them. (Acts 15:36, 41) Today, as the circuit servants make their visits, they too strengthen the congregations. They do this principally by giving attention to the spiritual needs of the brothers, by working with them in the field ministry and by checking the congregation organization.

The congregations and isolated groups visited by a circuit servant are termed a circuit. (1 Sam. 7:15, 16) The servant plans his route so as to visit each congregation in his circuit about once every four months, staying there for about a week on each occasion. Time is also set aside to serve publishers, pioneers, special pioneers and missionaries who are not living in congregation territory. Some isolated publishers may be assisted while he is serving a nearby congregation. If two groups are close together, he may decide to divide a week between them. But in the case of isolated pioneers, special pioneers and missionaries, he stays for a full week with them, holding meetings, helping them to improve their personal ministry and strengthening them spiritually for the work ahead.

Before the circuit servant visits your congregation, there is much that your overseer does by way of preparation to enable everyone to benefit to the full from the visit. When notice is received, about two months in advance, that the circuit servant is coming, the overseer may find it necessary to submit an order for additional magazines for the week of special activity, including whatever number the circuit servant has requested for himself. Handbills are also ordered for the public talk to be given. Locations from which field service will be carried out need to be selected and arrangements made for sleeping accommodations and meals for the circuit servant and his wife, if he is married. All this requires considerable time. Then, during the few weeks before the circuit servant's arrival, publishers are reminded of their appointments to go along in service with him; territory is selected to be worked by the group; pioneers, servants and the entire congregation are notified of special meetings and the times they will be held; congregation records are brought together for the circuit servant to check; and arrangements are made for the overseer and the circuit servant to visit publishers who may need spiritual help and encouragement.

When the circuit servant is with your congregation, all the regular meetings are held and some special ones too. It is a week of spiritual feasting. At the start of his visit, on Tuesday night, the Theocratic Ministry School and service meeting programs are conducted in somewhat shortened form (forty-five minutes each), followed by forty minutes of upbuilding counsel and Scriptural information from the circuit servant for the entire congregation. He also informs the congregation as to when and where the groups will meet for service during the week. Thursday night is set aside for the congregation book studies. Saturday night another special meeting is held for about an hour and fifteen minutes. At that time the circuit servant discusses with everyone present the spiritual condition of the congregation, their ministry and what he recommends for improvement. Part of the program is devoted to a stimulating review of new things learned through *The Watchtower* in recent months, and part is a Scriptural service talk. It is a most practical program. Then on Sunday, at the time scheduled by the congregation, the public talk is given (usually by the circuit servant), the *Watchtower* study is held and there is a beneficial concluding thirty-minute talk by the circuit servant. Certainly this spiritual provision is an evidence that Jehovah is providing for his people generously, just as he promised that he would do.—Isa. 65:13, 14; Mal. 3:10.

Ordinarily the regular congregation meetings are conducted by the appointed servant during the circuit servant's visit, and the circuit servant may offer private counsel to the conductor. However, at times the Society may request the circuit servant to conduct a certain meeting for one or more rounds of the circuit in order for the local servants to benefit from his example. Notification of any such adjustment is provided well in advance.

The week of his visit is also one of increased field service for the congregation, and the circuit servant will be pleased to go along with you. Would you like help to improve your house-to-house activity or your back-call ministry? Do you wish that you had a home Bible study to conduct or would you appreciate suggestions on the one you now have? We feel sure that the circuit servant can be of help to you, and that is one of the principal reasons why he visits your congregation.

Generally, the circuit servant plans to spend at least twenty-five hours in the service while he is with your congregation. Wednesday, Thursday and Friday are full days, calling for about six hours of service a day. Saturday and Sunday are scheduled with three or four hours of service each. One day may be set aside to feature magazine distribution, and service time on the other days is usually equally divided between house-to-house work and back-call or Bible study work. In order to accomplish the most work, the group starts early each morning, the time being determined by what is suitable in the locality. Could you arrange to make this a special week of service along with the circuit servant? We would like to suggest that you do. We know that Jehovah will richly reward your effort.

If the circuit servant is married and his wife travels with him, she, too, will be sharing in the field service. Usually she is a pioneer. No schedule is made for her to work with other publishers, but she may be glad to work with the sisters or other publishers, and, in that case, arrangements for it are made under the direction of her husband.

Considerable time is set aside during the week to give special attention to the appointed servants and pioneers. First, on Tuesday afternoon the circuit servant checks all the congregation records, both to be sure that they are being kept properly and to gather information that will help him to be of service to the congregation. Early Tuesday night there is a half-hour meeting with the servants to discuss what has been accomplished in the congregation since the circuit servant's previous visit and to outline what has been planned for the week. On Friday night, or at some other convenient time, the members of the committee meet with the circuit servant for an hour or two to discuss in detail the needs of the congregation, including the recommendations for servants, if necessary. And early Saturday night all the servants come together with the circuit servant to hear his comments on the needs of the congregation and to plan what they as servants will be doing to improve the spiritual condition of the congregation in the months ahead.

On Saturday afternoon there is a meeting with pioneers and special pioneers (and vacation pioneers are welcome, if they want to attend), to assist them with any problems and to offer beneficial counsel and suggestions. The circuit servant also makes it a point to work with each one of them in the service during the week. The Society is very much interested in these brothers and sisters who are spending so much of their time in the field ministry.

The circuit servant is keenly interested in the training of publishers and pioneers, with a view to their aiding others to become better qualified ministers of the good news. So, during the week of his visit, as he becomes acquainted with the capabilities of the various ones, he makes definite arrangements for the more capable ones to give personal assistance to those who need it in some feature of their service. He also takes note of any who have not been able to arrange their affairs to spend at least ten hours in the field service each month and, as opportunity affords, discusses the matter with them individually in a kind and constructive way. Where possible, he actually helps them to work out a schedule that fits their circumstances and that allows for a greater share in preaching the Kingdom message. Likewise, he has a keen interest in any who may be assisted to become vacation pioneers, regular pioneers, missionaries or members of a Bethel family. He is glad to discuss the prospects with them and, if possible, help them to see how to overcome any obstacles that may be in their way. If you wish that you could enjoy such service privileges, talk to him about it. His own experience in special service as well as his constant contact with many others who enjoy such privileges gives him a vast fund of practical knowledge from which to draw in offering suggestions for your benefit.

Full as the program of activity of the circuit servant is, he is still not too busy to take time to offer a helping hand to any "sheep" who may have strayed from the flock or become spiritually ill. He is, first of all, a shepherd of the flock of God. Usually he devotes an evening during the week to making visits on those in need of aid. Additionally, he may take a little time during the day to make calls on former publishers, if there is reason to believe they can be revived, and irregular ones who need to be strengthened. Sometimes keen interest in the spiritual welfare of other publishers requires calls too. Even when attention to these matters cuts down to some extent the hours that he is able to devote to the field ministry, he takes time for it, because he is deeply concerned about the welfare of all of Jehovah's people.

At the conclusion of his visit to each congregation, he makes out a Report on Congregation for the Society and leaves a copy of it with the overseer for the use of all the appointed servants. He also leaves a résumé of other suggestions that he has made to the servants during the week so that they will have them available for consultation and can follow through on them. Thus the benefits of his visit do not cease when he leaves.

Since the circuit servant travels to a different congregation each week, he usually does not have a permanent residence. In this respect he is like Jesus, who, though welcome in the homes of many lovers of the truth, had no place that he could really call his own, where he could lay his head at the close of a day. (Matt. 8:20; Mark 10:29, 30) It is the privilege of the local congregation to provide sleeping accommodations and meals for him and his wife, if possible. They endeavor to be, not a burden to the congregation, but, rather, a blessing. With that in mind, they urge those with whom they eat to keep in mind what Luke 10:38-42 says. Nothing elaborate is really necessary; instead, placing emphasis on spiritual matters is choosing the truly "good portion." The circuit servants have a full program of activity for the week and they need their sleep to care for it properly, so they are not able to spend much time visiting socially. But they do appreciate the hospitality of their Christian brothers and endeavor to reward them richly in a spiritual way.

At the close of each month when the circuit servant and his wife send their field service reports to the Society, they also submit a report on expenses incurred, provided they were not covered by the congregations. Such expenses for which the Society reimburses the circuit servant include transportation between congregations, but not expenses for getting around in the congregation territory. The Society will also cover food and lodging, if some congregations are not able to make provision. In addition, a small monthly allowance is sent for personal things, and the fact that they obtain literature at pioneer rates provides a little more to keep them going in the work. They have confidence that, as Jesus promised, if they seek continually the interests of Jehovah's kingdom, the material needs will be provided. —Luke 12:31.

The fine service provided by these mature brothers is greatly appreciated by Jehovah's people everywhere. It enables all of us to be better praisers of God, to enjoy close contact with the Society and to stand firm in the faith.

DISTRICT SERVANT

Another one of the traveling overseers of Jehovah's witnesses is the district servant. A number of circuits comprise a district, and, as the overseer of the district, the district servant regularly visits and works in the ministry with those who are circuit servants as well as serving as the principal speaker at circuit assemblies.

The district servant has a keen interest in the field ministry and, though he spends considerable time on organizational matters, he devotes eighty-five hours to house-to-house work, back-calls and Bible studies each month. Some months it may be less than that if there are many spiritually weak publishers who need special attention, but he always tries to set a zealous lead in the field work. If he is married, his wife, too, is a preacher of the Kingdom message, as all of Jehovah's witnesses are, and usually she is a pioneer, reporting at least a hundred hours in the field service each month.

The Society schedules the district servant to spend two weeks at a time in each circuit. One week he works with the circuit servant as he cares for his regular activity in serving a congregation. The other week he spends in the city where the circuit assembly is being held. His accommodations and expenses are cared for in the same manner as those of the circuit servant.

If your congregation is the one to be served by the circuit servant during the week that the district servant is with him, your overseer will be notified ahead of time so that adequate arrangements can be made. The circuit servant does his checking of records earlier than usual that week, and then on Tuesday afternoon he has the opportunity (along with his wife) to sit down with the district servant and discuss their ministry and any problems that may need attention. It is a special provision to build him up, so that he, in turn, can be a continued blessing to you. During the week the district servant will attend the meetings with the congregation, servants and pioneers. He observes how the circuit servant handles his work so that he can offer constructive suggestions for improvement. But he is not there simply to check up on the circuit servant; he is a fellow worker in the service of God, willing to share in what needs to be done and conscious of the importance of spiritually upbuilding and encouraging his brother. (Acts 11:23; Deut. 3:28) The district servant also shares to the full in the service arrangements for the week. He sets aside some time to work with the circuit servant and his wife, and there is also opportunity for you and others of the publishers to receive training from the district servant, just as you do from the circuit servant. Toward the end of the week, the district servant will give some talks to the congregation, taking the last half hour of the Saturday-night program and a half hour after the *Watchtower* study on Sunday.

The first part of the other week of the district servant's visit in the circuit is usually spent with the congregation in whose territory the semi-annual circuit assembly is to be held. Tuesday evening he gives an hour service talk to the congregation, and the next two days he spends in the field service with them. In the evenings he may show one of the Society's films in nearby congregations. In the meantime, the circuit servant usually is very busy with arrangements in connection with the forthcoming assembly.

The district servant, too, directs much of his attention toward assembly matters during the week because he is the assembly chairman. On Tuesday afternoon he gets together with the circuit servant to compile and discuss the information on the analysis report forms submitted by the congregations in the circuit, showing what they have been doing in the service, their meeting attendance, and so forth. This provides a basis for offering constructive counsel to the entire circuit. The assembly program itself usually begins on Friday night and extends through Sunday afternoon. Included in the arrangements is a meeting of congregation servants with the district and circuit servants on Saturday afternoon, followed by a stimulating meeting with those who are interested in pioneer service. The entire assembly is an occasion of spiritual refreshment, and extensive advertising is done to invite the public.

During the course of the assembly the district servant has opportunity to observe the operation of the assembly organization and to offer suggestions. The circuit servant is principally responsible for the assembly arrangements, obtaining the hall, immersion pool, and so forth. However, to assist him the Society appoints, on recommendation from the circuit servant, various permanent assembly personnel: an assembly servant, an assistant assembly servant and a public relations servant. They work closely with the circuit servant in supervising the assembly organization, so that the circuit servant can give more attention to the program. Other capable brothers, too, are designated by the circuit servant to care for various departments, and, if you would like to help, volunteers are always needed during the assembly to handle the great amount of work that is entailed in putting on an assembly.

Funds for operating circuit assemblies and defraying other circuit expenses are cared for by contributions from the brothers in the circuit, and for that reason contribution boxes are provided at the assembly. A circuit accounts servant appointed by the circuit servant keeps a record of this money and pays bills that have been approved by the circuit servant. If there is not enough money on hand to care for the initial expenses, the circuit servant may advise the congregations in the circuit of their privilege to assist with expenses. But usually after the first assembly in any circuit there are sufficient funds on hand to care for the initial expenses of the next assembly. Between assemblies this money is often deposited with the Society. However, if there is a deficit at the conclusion of the assembly, it is the responsibility of the congregation overseers to decide among themselves what contribution their congregations can make to the circuit fund to care for the expenses.

When any purchases of equipment for the circuit are made, when donations are made to the Society or there are other expenditures out of the ordinary, these matters are decided by the congregation overseers at their meeting on Saturday afternoon at the assembly. They are in position to consider what funds are available in the circuit, what expenses must be met in connection with the assembly, and so forth. They also know if their own congregation is in position to contribute toward extra expenses that may be incurred. Authorization of such expenditures is always put in writing in the form of a resolution, which is voted on only by the overseers. To keep the brothers informed of the standing of the accounts and how the money that they have contributed is being used, a brief statement of receipts and disbursements is made up for each assembly and read to all the brothers by the circuit servant.

Knowing to some extent how the circuit assembly organization functions should sharpen your appreciation for it. The provision of these assemblies is to keep you spiritually strong. Be sure that you always benefit from them to the full.

ZONE SERVANT

Even branch servants, who have general oversight of the congregations and the preaching work in an entire country or group of lands, are visited and assisted by other responsible servants in Jehovah's organization. The president of the Society periodically visits all the branch offices to inspect them and handle problems. But in addition to his visits, arrangements are made for persons who are appointed by the Society through the president to visit the branch offices and printing plants of the Society as well as all the missionary homes. These brothers are known as zone servants.

They check the records of each branch, analyze its oversight of the congregations and what is being accomplished in the field service. They attend congregation meetings with these brothers and work with them in the field ministry. Usually these zone servants are themselves branch servants, so they can appreciate the problems that arise and work them out with the brothers whom they are serving. Later, when they are back in the branch offices where they are assigned as branch servants, a zone servant visits there and provides the same service for them. So, there is, indeed, an interchange of encouragement. Everyone in the organization, the congregation publisher and the responsible overseer alike, is strengthened with a sense of interdependency, just as the various parts of a human body serve for the common good of the whole body. And as each one in the organization is drawn close to his fellow servants in loving unity, he is also brought closer to Jesus Christ, the head of the Christian congregation, and to Jehovah God, whose spirit permeates the entire organization and whose Word guides its operation in harmony with his righteous purpose. —1 Cor. 12:12-31; Eph. 1:22, 23; Prov. 3:5, 6.

CHAPTER 9

Financing the Preaching Work

A QUESTION frequently asked by persons who are newly associated with Jehovah's witnesses is, Who provides the money for carrying on this work? The answer is that Jehovah's witnesses everywhere have a part in it.

There is never any solicitation of funds, but the brothers are aware of the great amount of work being done by the Society in connection with the preaching of the good news of the Kingdom in all the earth, they know that it requires money, and they want to have a share in providing it. They are free to send voluntary contributions to the nearest branch office of the Watch Tower Bible and Tract Society. They are like God's servants in ancient times who brought, 'everyone whose heart impelled him, a voluntary offering to Jehovah.' (Ex. 35:20-29) Most of the donations received are in relatively small amounts, but these, when added together, provide enough to keep the work going. (Luke 21:1-4) Some gifts are received from estates, under wills of Jehovah's witnesses.

It is a privilege to share in this way in furthering the work in all parts of the earth, and none need feel that what they are able to offer is too little to be worthwhile. As 2 Corinthians 8:12 says: "If the readiness is there first, it is especially acceptable according to what a person has, not according to what a person does not have." Contributions are received by the Society from individuals, congregations and circuits. The Society appreciates the donations that are made and acknowledges them.

None of this money is used to enrich individuals; it is all put to work to advance the preaching of the good news of the Kingdom. It is used to build and maintain printing plants where Bible literature is produced; and the full-time workers who care for this work are supplied with "sustenance and covering" and a small allowance for personal expenses. (1 Tim. 6:8) Others who are devoting all their time and energy to the ministry as missionaries, special pioneers, circuit and district servants are also given assistance so that they will have the food and shelter required as they carry on their work. Additionally, literature is provided at less than cost to all these full-time workers as well as to pioneers and vacation pioneers to help defray their expenses. This is made possible by contributions to the Society from you and your brothers everywhere.

In addition to these contributions to the Society, the individuals associated with each congregation support their own Kingdom Hall and care for any other expenses locally. No collection is ever taken, but contribution boxes are provided at our meeting places so that each one can have a part "just as he has resolved in his heart."—2 Cor. 9:7.

Furthermore, you generously contribute time and effort to the preaching work in your territory. You are willing to bear your own expenses in this, and you expect no money in return for the assistance that you offer to those with whom you study the Bible. As is true of Jehovah's witnesses everywhere, you apply the instructions of Jesus Christ, who said: "You received free, give free." (Matt. 10:8) The appointed servants in your congregation view things in the same way. Though they do much extra work in caring for the congregation, they are paid no salary for this. They serve because of love for Jehovah and for his "sheep." With you, they are glad to expend themselves in Jehovah's service. Yes, Jehovah's people find happiness in giving.—Acts 20:35.

CHAPTER 10

Keeping the Congregation Clean

NOT only the appointed servants, but every one of Jehovah's witnesses should be deeply interested in maintaining the peace and unity of the congregation. (1 Pet. 3:10, 11) It is of primary importance that we be at peace with God and that we actively demonstrate our love for him. (2 John 6) But the Bible is frank in saying that "he who does not love his brother, whom he has seen, cannot be loving God, whom he has not seen." (1 John 4:20) So we cannot honestly profess to love Jehovah God if we are harboring animosity toward our Christian brothers and sisters. Jesus Christ said: "By this all will know that you are my disciples, if you have love among yourselves." (John 13:35) Failure to demonstrate that quality would mean that one was not walking in Jesus' footsteps.

Even when someone offends us, love ought to move us to be forgiving. On this the Scriptures counsel: "Continue putting up with one another and forgiving one another freely if anyone has a cause for complaint against another. Even as Jehovah freely forgave you, so do you also." (Col. 3:13) This does not mean that Christians approve of wrongdoing, but they realize that all are imperfect, and they deal kindly with one another, just as they want God to deal with them.—Matt. 6:12, 14, 15; 18:21-35.

So, when difficulties arise between members of the congregation, mature Christians do not vengefully seek to cause injury to the one who injured them. (1 Pet. 3:8, 9) Nor do they coolly refuse to talk to him anymore. (1 Cor. 13:4, 5; Eph. 4:26) Where possible, they simply overlook offenses against them, especially so when they realize that they have not been committed with malice. —Eph. 4:32; Prov. 19:11.

But what if the sin committed was a serious matter? What if it has caused a serious breach between you and the other person? Or what if you believe that it might result in harm to other individuals in the congregation simply to forget the incident? What steps should you take?

Gossiping to others is not the answer; that would only make the situation worse. Furthermore, the Bible does not say that you should first ask your Christian overseer to talk to the offender. You have a responsibility. At Matthew 18:15 it is written: "If your brother commits a sin, go lay bare his fault [reprove him] between you and him alone. If he listens to you, you have gained your brother." If the wrongdoer knew that he had done wrong, was repentant and had taken steps to set matters right, of course, this would usually not be necessary. But when he does not initiate that action, the Bible admonishes you as the one against whom the sin was committed to approach the wrongdoer. This is to be done, not in an angry frame of mind, but to 'gain your brother.' When the approach is made in a kindly way, usually a reconciliation is readily brought about. Thus the wrongdoer is helped to bring his life back into line with God's Word. But what if the difficulty persists and does not appear to be something that you can dismiss?

Take the next step, the one set out at Matthew 18:16: "If he does not listen, take along with you one or two more, in order that at the mouth of two or three witnesses every matter may be established." That does not mean that you should round up sympathizers, persons who you feel sure will side in with you. Seek the aid of mature Christian brothers. It may be that, while the offender was previously inclined to brush the matter aside as of little account or was actually inclined to continue in a course contrary to Christian principles, now he will be impressed with the seriousness of the situation. The mature brothers whom you take with you may offer helpful Scriptural counsel, and perhaps there will be favorable response to it. Everyone concerned will be glad to have the matter rectified. On the other hand, if there is a belligerent rejection of what the Scriptures say, if there is a determination to continue in an unchristian course, there will be two or three witnesses to this. In such a case, when the person does not listen, rejecting all efforts at reconciliation and spurning the counsel of God's Word, Jesus admonished, "speak to the congregation." (Matt. 18:17) That is, to the "older men" in the congregation who are responsible servants.

Seldom will it be necessary to carry the matter this far, though. Usually difficulties can be settled between the two persons involved. Your accepting the responsibility to handle problems in this loving way is a contribution to the spiritual welfare of the congregation.

There are other important contributions that you personally can make to the spiritual health of the congregation too. You can help to keep the organization morally clean, free of corrupting influences. All of us can do this, and we should, not leaving it to the overseer as if it were all his problem. If we maintain fine conduct, observers are moved to glorify God. But if a person engages in loose conduct, he causes the way of the truth to be spoken of abusively. (1 Pet. 2:12; 2 Pet. 2:2) When you resist temptation to wrongdoing you are contributing to the moral cleanness of the organization. The same is true when you refuse to feed your mind on ideas that stimulate wrong desires. Parents, by properly training and disciplining their children so that they walk in the paths of righteousness, contribute to the fine reputation of Jehovah's organization. So do younger persons, by obedience to their parents and by refusing to imitate the world and its ways. When you take care to teach interested persons the Bible's high moral standards before they get baptized, this, too, acts to keep the organization clean. These are things that it is most important to do, so that the spirit of God may continue to operate freely on the congregation.—1 Cor. 5:5.

HELP FOR THOSE OVERTAKEN IN SIN

Nevertheless, it may happen that someone who is a dedicated and baptized witness of Jehovah gets involved in unchristian conduct or he may be doing things that can easily lead to trouble. He may not even realize the seriousness of the situation. What can be done about it? Galatians 6:1, 2 says: "Brothers, even though a man takes some false step before he is aware of it, you who have spiritual qualifications try to restore such a man in a spirit of mildness, as you each keep an eye on yourself, for fear you also may be tempted. Go on carrying the burdens of one another, and thus fulfill the law of the Christ." So, the appointed servants, and perhaps other spiritually mature ones, will lovingly endeavor to help the erring one to view things in Jehovah's way and to make straight paths for his feet.

More often, though, a baptized Christian knows what the Bible says about conduct that is pleasing to God, and if he has become involved in anything that is Scripturally wrong he is aware of it. True, what he did may not have been premeditated; he may have been overcome in temptation before he realized it. But now, as he looks back, he knows that he has been displeasing to Jehovah. What should he do? He ought to go to God humbly in prayer through Jesus Christ, confess his wrong and seek forgiveness. (Ps. 32:5; 1 Tim. 2:5) Then he should take steps to avoid any circumstances that will lead to repetition of the wrong. All of us are imperfect and fall short of God's standard of righteousness. (Rom. 3:23) That is why Jesus, in teaching his followers how to pray, told them to include in their petition to God this request: "Forgive us our debts, as we also have forgiven our debtors."—Matt. 6:12.

When serious difficulties begin to arise, however, it is also wise to seek the counsel of a mature Christian brother. That brother could be the congregation overseer or one of the other members of the committee. Additionally, in some places, there are other men of comparable maturity in the congregation, and they, too, may be approached with confidence when one is in need of help. Jehovah, who knows our weaknesses, has lovingly arranged for us to have help from these brothers when we need it the most. Note what James 5:14-16 states in connection with this: "Is there anyone [spiritually] sick among you?

Let him call the older men of the congregation to him, and let them pray over him, greasing him with oil in the name of Jehovah. And the prayer of faith will make the indisposed one well, and Jehovah will raise him up. Also, if he has committed sins, it will be forgiven him. Therefore openly confess your sins to one another and pray for one another, that you may get healed. A righteous man's supplication, when it is at work, has much force."

The assistance that mature men can render is a provision that Jehovah has made for our good, and not just an arrangement whereby certain ones are appointed to check up on what everyone else does. Obviously, when a person commits grievous sins it is evidence of spiritual weakness. A person in this position needs help to overcome his difficulties, and is wise if he asks for that help.

There is grave danger in not asking for assistance. If a brother in difficulty fails to do so, he may just find that he will become habituated in a course of sin until he becomes irreformable or, even if he does not repeat the wrong, he may draw away from association with Jehovah's organization for fear that someone may learn of his wrong act. (Prov. 18:1) How much better for the erring one to acknowledge humbly that there are times when he needs help and so avail himself of the loving provision Jehovah has made!

Remember what is recorded at Proverbs 28:13: "He that is covering over his transgressions will not succeed, but he that is confessing and leaving them will be shown mercy." So if someone has fallen into sinful conduct and is really sorry about it, he shows that, not by covering over his transgression, but by confessing it, seeking help, and thereafter carefully avoiding the circumstances that might lead to a repetition of the wrong. In this way he can be restored spiritually and again enjoy Jehovah's warm smile of approval.

Regardless of the spiritual assistance that a mature brother may give to one in difficulty, however, there are certain types of cases that always should be brought to the attention of the congregation committee. These are lying, stealing, drunkenness and other serious offenses when they have been *committed repeatedly*. Such repeated sin is a serious matter, but if the wrongdoer has voluntarily confessed and sincerely wants to do what is right in Jehovah's eyes, it may be that he can be helped.

Certain other cases that may not involve repetition of a sin should also be brought to the attention of the committee. These include cases of sexual immorality involving other persons, whether committed by adults or dedicated and baptized minors, and other serious wrongdoing that has become public knowledge or that may readily become a matter of discussion in the congregation.

HEARINGS BEFORE THE COMMITTEE

Those servants in each congregation who are charged with responsibility to hear matters such as these constitute the congregation committee. Usually this judicial committee, all of whom are males, is made up of the congregation servant, the assistant congregation servant and the Bible study servant. However, on occasion one of the brothers may ask to step aside in a certain case, in order to assure impartiality, and then the other two select a third mature brother to complete the committee to hear the case. These qualified brothers are desirous of helping to bring about the spiritual restoration of any who have stumbled due to imperfection but who are sincerely repentant, and they are also keenly aware of their obligation to protect the organization against any who may be "turning the undeserved kindness of our God into an excuse for loose conduct" and who seek to corrupt the clean, trusting people of God.—Jude 4.

If you personally are ever a witness to serious wrongdoing on the part of a dedicated and baptized member of the congregation, or if you come to know of it, loyalty to Jehovah and his organization should move you to bring it to the attention of the responsible servants. (Ps. 31:23) It is no real kindness to the wrongdoer to conceal his unchristian conduct; it may only harden him in sin to the point where he cannot turn back, and so lead to his everlasting destruction. Certainly it shows no love for Jehovah God or his people when one becomes a party to wickedness by concealing those who practice it. One who loves righteousness and is truly loyal to God will courageously step forward and expose the sinful conduct and fearlessly testify to the truth of the matter before the committee when called on to do so. —Lev. 5:1; Eph. 4:24; Luke 1:74, 75.

Whenever a charge of serious wrongdoing is made against a person, arrangements are made for the congregation judicial committee to hear the matter. Notification of the time of the meeting and its purpose is sent in writing to the one against whom the charge has been made. He is informed what his course of action is supposed to have been and he is treated in a kind manner. If he does not show up on the date set by the committee, then the committee considerately endeavors to find out what date would be convenient to him. The person is given full opportunity to make a statement and to present witnesses on his behalf before the committee, just as the committee is willing to hear other witnesses and those who are making charges. But refusal to come to the hearing, even the second time, will not prevent the committee from taking action if the evidence is clearly established.—Num. 16:12-14, 25-33.

Judgment of matters affecting the lives of dedicated servants of Jehovah carries with it a great responsibility, and, for that reason, the committee is obligated to be sure that it has all the facts before it renders its decision. (1 Tim. 5:21; Prov. 18:13; Deut. 13:12-14) For a matter to be established as true, there must be two or three witnesses. (1 Tim. 5:19; Deut. 19:15) These cannot be persons who are simply repeating what they have heard from someone else; they must be witnesses of the things concerning which they testify. No action is taken if there is just one witness; it is not that the brothers discredit the testimony, but the Bible requires that, unless the wrongdoer himself confesses his sin, the facts must be substantiated by two or three witnesses in these serious matters.

However, if a brother or a sister confesses a sin committed with another brother or sister and there are no witnesses to prove it, would not the acceptance of that one's confession of guilt also obligate the committee to judge guilty the one charged as party to the sin? In such a case the one confessing is urged to follow the advice at Matthew 18:15-17, and the brothers make sure that each of the steps outlined there is taken. If the accused denies the charge throughout, and there is no further evidence to prove him guilty, then the Scriptures do not authorize those doing the judging to declare him guilty. He may be guilty, and, if he is, Jehovah knows that, and in time will see that the truth is brought to light. (1 Tim. 5:24) At the same time, adhering to the Scriptural rule prevents any injustice. But what of the one who confessed the sinful conduct? This person is guilty of either the sin confessed or of lying and bearing false witness against a fellow Christian, and, if thus guilty would, if repentant, be put on probation.

If, in the course of a hearing before the committee, the required witnesses are available and it is definitely established that the accused did commit a sin warranting disfellowshiping, the committee endeavors to determine if there is basis for mercy. If there is not, then they are Scripturally obligated to disfellowship the wrongdoer. (1 Cor. 5:9-13) Although they may feel sorry for the wrongdoer, this is not by itself a sound basis for mercy. The basis for mercy lies in sincere repentance on the part of the wrongdoer. (2 Chron. 7:14; Isa. 55:7) He may say that he is sorry, but is he really cut to the heart over his sin and, out of love for Jehovah and his organization, does he really want to avoid any repetition of his wrong course? (Ezek. 18:30, 31) If a person manifests indifference about the situation, or professes repentance but then persists in his wrong conduct, the divine requirements of justice may not be sidestepped.

DISFELLOWSHIPING

When anyone is disfellowshiped from the Christian congregation, a resolution is drawn up by the judicial committee and presented to the congregation, informing them that the individual has been disfellowshiped for conduct unbecoming a Christian. The congregation is not invited to vote on this resolution. The committee is responsible for acting on behalf of the entire congregation, because they have made the investigation. Those who love Jehovah's law and his righteousness will accept the decision made and not complain against those responsible for handling the matter. (Num. 16:41-50; Ps. 119:29, 30) Notification of the decision is sent by the committee to the Society, giving the date the action was taken, the grounds and evidence for it, and each member of the committee signs the letter. The Society then sends a disfellowshiped person's card to the congregation, which is retained in the congregation's file. Of course, if one who is disfellowshiped believes that the action of the committee was improper, he may appeal to the Society, but in doing so he should submit a copy of his letter to the committee of the congregation that took the action.

Being disfellowshiped is a serious matter. It means that one is expelled from the congregation; he can no longer enjoy the warm fellowship of faithful Christians and he is no longer recognized as a member of the congregation. The faithful members of the congregation therefore "quit mixing in company" with such a person. (1 Cor. 5:11, 13) Any baptized person who deliberately chooses a course of immoral conduct shows that he now rejects the teachings of the Bible, just as much so as one who openly teaches others contrary to what the Scriptures say about the identity of God, the provision of the ransom, the resurrection, and so forth. (Titus 3:10, 11) Concerning such persons God's Word counsels: "Everyone that pushes ahead and does not remain in the teaching of the Christ does not have God. . . . If anyone comes to you and does not bring this teaching, never receive him into your homes or say a greeting to him. For he that says a greeting to him is a sharer in his wicked works." (2 John 9-11) In faithfulness to God, none in the congregation should greet such persons when meeting them in public nor should they welcome these into their homes. Even blood relatives who do not live in the same home, valuing spiritual relationships more, avoid contact with them just as much as possible. And those who may be members of the same household with a disfellowshiped person cease sharing spiritual fellowship with the wrongdoer. In this way the evildoer is made to feel the enormity of his wrong, and, at the same time, Jehovah upholds the good name of his organization and protects the spiritual well-being of those in it.

If a disfellowshiped person wants to attend meetings to get himself restored spiritually, he is not prohibited from attending public meetings in the Kingdom Hall, provided he conducts himself properly. None will greet him, of course, and he may not attend any meetings held in private homes. The congregation will not assign him any territory in which to preach, nor will any service reports be accepted from him. If he wants to read the Society's publications, however, he may obtain copies for personal use. Perhaps what he reads will help to correct his thinking, soften his heart and move him to turn back to Jehovah.

REINSTATEMENT

If a disfellowshiped person comes to his senses, repents of his sins and manifests this beyond a reasonable doubt over a period of time, he may appeal in writing to the congregation servant for reinstatement. No plea for reinstatement will be considered for at least a year after disfellowshiping, and in some cases even more. However, if sufficient time has elapsed, the committee may call him in and listen to what he has to say. If they are convinced that he has had a change of heart and has had it for a considerable period of time, and if they believe that Jehovah God has forgiven him because of his contrite heart, and if they see that he is humbly desirous of doing Jehovah's will, then there is a Scriptural basis for them to consider reinstatement. But if he has only very recently done anything about changing his ways, or seeks constantly to justify himself and does not show a humble spirit, then no proper basis for reinstatement exists.

In those cases where the committee decides that the Scriptures authorize them to reinstate a person, they draw up a resolution to that effect and read it to the congregation as notification that the individual has been reinstated. They also advise the Society of this action, returning the disfellowshiped person's card, bearing the date of reinstatement and the congregation servant's signature. The formerly disfellowshiped person can then be accepted back into the congregation as a brother. (2 Cor. 2:6-8) However, to test further his fitness to be back in the congregation and to afford opportunity to strengthen him spiritually, the committee will put him on probation, usually for at least a year, setting out certain reasonable restrictions regarding his conduct. During this time he may share freely in all features of the field ministry and he may comment in meetings, at the discretion of the conductor. However, until the termination of the probation period he may not appear on the platform at meetings for any reason other than to give student talks, nor will he be called on to represent the congregation in prayer. He will be advised when the probation ends, though no announcement of this is made to the congregation.

One who is disfellowshiped is cut off, not only from the local congregation where he has been attending meetings, but from all the congregations of Jehovah's people everywhere. However, since the circumstances that led to the disfellowshiping are best known locally, the congregation that disfellowships is also the one that reinstates, even though the wrongdoer moves to another congregation. The congregation where he is currently associated may hear the person's plea and make its recommendation, with reasons, to the congregation that first handled the case, but the decision will be made by the now-existing committee of the first congregation. Similarly, the congregation that imposes probation is the one to terminate it.

PROBATION

Not all cases of wrongdoing that are brought to the attention of the committee lead to disfellowshiping. Sometimes all that is needed is good counsel. Even if the sin was a serious one but there is basis for mercy because of the willing confession and sincere repentance of the dedicated and baptized person, and particularly so if it was a first offense, they may put the erring one on probation. Such probations are not usually announced, unless the wrongdoing has become generally known. It is up to the committee to decide if any announcement will be made. But if the person holds any appointment from the Society, whether as a servant or a pioneer, the Society is notified.

Ordinarily the probation period runs for a year, during which time the committee observes the conduct of the person and provides needed assistance to strengthen him spiritually. If the individual is put on probation because of committing an act of sexual immorality with another person or if the probation for any wrongdoing is announced to the congregation, his privileges of service in the congregation will be restricted during the probation period. He may not continue as an appointed servant in the congregation during the time of such a probation, nor may he appear on the platform at meetings for any reason other than to give student talks, and he will not be called on to represent the congregation in prayer. However, he may share in the field ministry and comment in meetings, at the discretion of the conductor. Probation terms never include restrictions on eating or drinking nor do they require performance of certain service requirements, though appropriate counsel may be given. Yet if bad associations have led to the offense, these may be reasonably restricted to protect the individual from circumstances that might lead to a repetition of the sin. (1 Cor. 15:33; 2 Cor. 6:17) If the probation is not because of sexual immorality and no announcement is made to the congregation, it may not be necessary to restrict the individual's service privileges, but that is something that the committee may decide. During the probation period provision is made for one of the committee to spend some time with the person each month to discuss Scriptural information appropriate to the person's needs, with a view to building him up spiritually.—1 Thess. 5:14.

If some person who is regularly associated with the congregation, but is not a dedicated and baptized Witness, gets involved in grossly unchristian conduct, this is not ignored. Since the unbaptized person is really not a member of the congregation, he is not officially disfellowshiped from it or put on probation. Nevertheless, no one who seeks to corrupt Jehovah's people is permitted to carry on his activity unrestrained. If a person simply does not know the Bible's requirements, kindly personal counsel may help him to straighten out his paths. But if he does not love righteousness and is unrepentant, announcement can be made to the congregation to put them on guard against him.

Should it be that reports of openly reproachful conduct on the part of a baptized member of the congregation reach the committee, even though committed by one who no longer comes to meetings, it is their duty to inquire into the situation. One is not relieved of accountability simply by ceasing to associate with Jehovah's people; the obligations that attend dedication and baptism are for life. If such a one deliberately chooses to live immorally, for example, or to take up false religious practices, he brings reproach on Jehovah's organization, misrepresenting it before friends and acquaintances who know that he was baptized as a Witness. So it is the obligation of the committee to clear the congregation of any share in the responsibility for the wrong by taking definite action to expel such a person.—2 Cor. 7:11.

In the case of wrongdoing by minor children, the dedicated and baptized parents bear the responsibility for handling the situation; particularly is it the father's responsibility. (Eph. 6:4; Col. 3:20) It is up to them to decide what should be done to make amends for their child's wrongs. If they feel that certain restrictions should be placed on the child for a time, that is for them to work out. (Heb. 12:9) If the conduct engaged in by the child put the congregation in a bad light, then they ought to tell the committee what they have done to handle the situation. But as long as they are shouldering the responsibility, the committee is not going to try to step in and do the job, even in the case of dedicated and baptized minors. However, if any parents let their dedicated children engage in loose conduct and fail to keep them in check, the congregation committee may inquire into the situation, but they endeavor to do this through the parents, encouraging them to shoulder the responsibility for the children. Yet, if the parents continue to fail to take firm hold of the situation, even after loving counsel has been offered to them, then the congregation committee will take what steps are needed in connection with the children to keep the congregation clean. Similarly, if a dedicated and baptized minor persists in serious wrongdoing, refusing to submit to probation imposed by his parents, the congregation will take action to disfellowship the persistently sinning youth.

So it is seen that in the case of a youth whose parents, or at least one of them, are members of the congregation, probation may be handled largely within the family circle. The committee should regularly be informed of what is being done in cases of serious wrong, but, as long as the parents take the matter in hand and the youth submits to their probation, it is proper for the parents to care for the situation. Likewise, in the case of a married person who sins against that one's mate by committing adultery (and only for this offense). If the offender was overtaken in weakness but now is grief-stricken and confesses and asks forgiveness of the innocent mate, a period of probation may be imposed on the erring one. The committee should examine the case to decide if the erring one is truly repentant and whether there is a basis for merciful probation. If there is such a basis, then the faithful mate may institute and supervise the probation, and a member of the committee will simply offer suitable help from time to time to assist in building up the erring one spiritually.

Our learning to live now in harmony with Jehovah's requirements, maintaining cleanness in teaching and conduct, is preparation for life in God's new system of things. Therefore it is vital for each one of us to impress God's righteous precepts on his mind and heart. Accurate knowledge of God's law will safeguard us against bringing great grief upon both ourselves and others because of ignorance, and love for what Jehovah shows us to be right will motivate us to act in harmony with it.

CHAPTER 11

Opportunities to Share in Special Privileges of Service

ANYONE who truly finds his "exquisite delight in Jehovah" rejoices at the prospect of added privileges of service. (Ps. 37:4; Isa. 58:14) He finds genuine pleasure in doing the will of God and is glad to take on additional responsibilities.

To him it is no unpleasant burden but is the work that, more than anything else, he wants to do. —Ps. 40:8.

The importance of moving ahead, reaching out for increased knowledge and improving the quality of service that we personally offer to God, is highlighted repeatedly in the Scriptures. The apostle Peter urged fellow believers to "go on growing in the undeserved kindness and knowledge of our Lord." (2 Pet. 3:18) Hebrew Christians were counseled to "press on to maturity." (Heb. 6:1) The brothers in Corinth were admonished to "widen out," to demonstrate by their actions their concern for other people. (2 Cor. 6: 13) Paul told the Philippians that his ministry on their behalf was 'for their advancement,' and he urged Timothy to apply himself to the ministry, that his "advancement may be manifest to all persons." (Phil. 1:25; 1 Tim. 4:15) Because of the fine advancement made by some, the same apostle felt moved to write to the congregation of the Thessalonians: "We are obligated to give God thanks always for you, brothers, as it is fitting, because your faith is growing exceedingly and the love of each and all of you is increasing one toward the other."—2 Thess. 1:3.

The need for us to show increase in the use of what has been entrusted to us was forcefully illustrated by Jesus in a parable. He told of a certain man of noble birth who was about to travel abroad to secure kingly power and who called his servants to him and, entrusting each one with a mina, he told them to do business with it. "Eventually when he got back after having secured the kingly power, he commanded to be called to him these slaves to whom he had given the silver money, in order to ascertain what they had gained by business activity. Then the first one presented himself, saying, 'Lord, your mina gained ten minas.' So he said to him, 'Well done, good slave!

Because in a very small matter you have proved
yourself faithful, hold authority over ten cities.'
Now the second came, saying, 'Your mina, Lord,
made five minas.' He said to this one also, 'You,
too, be in charge of five cities.'" Another slave,
although he had not lost his mina, showed no increase, and he was judged unfaithful and what he
had was taken from him. (Luke 19:12-26) Christ
Jesus is the One to whom Jehovah has given kingly power and he has entrusted the privilege of
participating in the ministry as Kingdom witnesses to all his followers, saying: "Go therefore
and make disciples of people of all the nations."
—Matt. 28:19.

By this parable Jesus shows that approval is
obtained, not by merely retaining what has been
entrusted to us, but by working with it in such a
way that we show an increase. Why so? Because
this indicates a right and good heart condition. As
Jesus explained in his parable of the sower: "As
for the one sown upon the fine soil, this is the one
hearing the word and getting the sense of it, who
really does bear fruit and produces, this one a
hundredfold, that one sixty, the other thirty."
(Matt. 13:23) One whose heart proves to be "fine
soil" is receptive to God's Word and responsive to
the direction of His organization, and, as a result,
God blesses the work of his hands with increase.

To show an increase we must apply ourselves,
seeking to grow in a knowledge of Bible truth,
availing ourselves of provisions made to help us
improve our personal ability and participating
zealously in the field ministry. At no point should
we become complacent, adopting the attitude that
we have done our part and now we will let others
carry the load. Though our physical capabilities
may limit us, if our hearts are filled to overflowing
with gratitude to God we will continue to serve
wholeheartedly. Additional opportunities to advance the interests of pure worship will always be

to us, in the full sense of the word, *privileges of service*. We will respond to the Scriptural admonition: "Stay awake, stand firm in the faith, carry on as men, grow mighty. Let all your affairs take place with love."—1 Cor. 16:13, 14.

Every one of Jehovah's witnesses, whether recently baptized or with many years of experience in the ministry, ought to have in mind enlarging his privileges of service. Each one, being progressive, would do well to have a goal in the ministry toward which he is working—a goal that can be attained in a reasonable length of time and that will serve as a stepping-stone to further advancement.

Basic to any real progress is regularity in participation. Do you have a share in the field ministry regularly each week? It is something that we all should endeavor to do. That is not a stepping-stone that can be skipped over, with the thought that other goals in the ministry can readily be reached even though this one is ignored. It deserves serious consideration and careful planning. There should be definite time set aside in your schedule each week for the field ministry. Having taken that step, you will find that the others are easier, and your enjoyment of the service will grow as you take each one of them.

There are many features of service in which you can engage, and progressively you will want to include all of them in your regular program of activity. If you are physically able to do so, you no doubt engage in the house-to-house work, as did Jesus and his apostles. (Acts 20:20; 1 Cor. 11:1) But do you also make back-calls on each one who manifests interest in the good news? Are you regularly conducting a home Bible study? No doubt it was through such service that you were enabled to come to a knowledge of the truth, and this should help you to appreciate the importance of having a regular, weekly share in these features of service to aid others onto the way of life. No farmer goes into his field to sow seed and then abandons it, allowing the weeds to take over. He patiently cultivates, clears out weeds and then works diligently to gather in the harvest. (Jas. 5:7; 1 Cor. 3:9) So it should be with your ministry. Having talked to people about God's purposes and placed literature with them, now you ought to cultivate the interest, patiently clear out obstacles to spiritual growth and aid them to produce "righteous fruit, which is through Jesus Christ, to God's glory and praise." (Phil. 1:11) If you are not regularly participating in these important aspects of the ministry, make it a matter of prayer to God, ask one of the appointed servants for aid and apply yourself diligently to the work. If you are already sharing in these privileges of service, why not consider how you can improve your effectiveness so as to accomplish more in the time you do devote to the field ministry? As your progress in the ministry becomes more manifest, the rewarding joy that goes with such a productive course will be yours.—Matt. 25:23.

The need for mature ministers, those who are ready and willing to accept increased responsibility, is great. How many are there associated with your congregation who, due to lack of appreciation, are devoting only a few hours to the field service each month and showing little in the way of increase? They need the loving assistance of zealous ones who are willing to sit down and study with them, help them to prepare sermons, aid them to improve their handling of problems met in the house-to-house work, go along with them on back-calls and help them to establish home Bible studies. They need personal instruction and encouragement. "We, though, who are strong ought to bear the weaknesses of those not strong, and not to be pleasing ourselves. Let each of us please his neighbor in what is good for his upbuilding." (Rom. 15:1, 2) Are you taking steps to make room in your ministry for this special privilege of service?

Productive field ministry has resulted in increase in the number of congregations, and this too opens opportunities for special service. Over a period of years thousands of additional congregation overseers and tens of thousands of ministerial servants are needed. Yet this is not all. In nearly every congregation there are openings for mature brothers to enlarge their privileges by taking on servant responsibilities, for many of those now assigned hold two or three positions. The apostle Paul commends those who are reaching out for such service, saying: "If any man is reaching out for an office of overseer, he is desirous of a fine work." (1 Tim. 3:1) It is not honor that they seek; they are desirous of work, a fine work; they want to do more in Jehovah's service and to be of greater service to their Christian brothers.

As we have already seen in the parable of the minas, a person shows himself worthy of being entrusted with greater responsibility by proving himself faithful and showing increase in caring for what has already been put into his care. If he is diligent and acquires skill in the house-to-house ministry, makes back-calls, conducts progressive Bible studies, is regular in all the available features of the service, handles each assignment on the congregation meetings in an upbuilding manner, goes out of his way to do things for his brothers, and manifests in all that he does the fruits of God's spirit, he is showing by his faithful course that he qualifies for additional privileges of service. In time he may be appointed as a ministerial servant, and when he has gained experience in connection with the work of each of the ministerial servants, he may, when the need arises, be appointed as congregation overseer. Of these, some who are spiritually qualified, and circumstantially able, may even be entrusted with the responsibilities of circuit or district servants. They receive such appointments, not because they have gained the attention of some prominent brother, but because they have won the approval of God. Having proved themselves faithful in little things, they are blessed by God with greater responsibilities. (Ps. 75:5-7; Luke 16:10) Does the course that you are pursuing in the ministry give evidence that you are reaching out for these privileges of service?

There are other opportunities to share in special privileges of service too. As we consider them together, perhaps you will find that they are within your reach.

SERVING WHERE THE NEED IS GREATER

No matter where you live, there is work to be done in Jehovah's service. Even though some territories have been covered repeatedly, continued preaching makes the name of the true God more prominent and aids those who sigh and groan over the detestable things being done in Christendom to embrace Jehovah's loving provision for salvation. (Ezek. 9:4; 2 Pet. 3:15) There is no reason for ministers of God who live in such territories to slow down in their service.

Yet there are places where the need for Kingdom preachers is greater. In some areas the territory is not covered even once a year. Persons living there have had only limited opportunity to hear God's Word. As reported in the *Yearbook of Jehovah's Witnesses*, there are even locations where so many persons want to study the Bible that the publishers there cannot care for them all. When we view those areas we are moved to say, as did Jesus: "Yes, the harvest is great, but the workers are few. Therefore, beg the Master of the harvest to send out workers into his harvest." (Matt. 9:37, 38) The call for workers in the harvest is loud and clear. No other work being done on earth is as important as this urgent work of witnessing that Jehovah is having done under angelic supervision.—Rev. 14:6, 7.

Many have heard the call and have responded. They have felt as did the apostle Paul and his companions when Paul had a vision of a Macedonian man who was beseeching him and saying: "Step over into Macedonia and help us." "Now as soon as he had seen the vision," the account continues, "we sought to go forth into Macedonia, drawing the conclusion that God had summoned us to declare the good news to them." (Acts 16:9, 10) So, today, those who have responded to the call feel that it is God who has summoned them and that it is he who, through his organization, has showed them this open door leading to enlarged service.

Some who enjoy this service do so along with their congregation, devoting full weekends during the summer months to preaching in territories designated by the Society as being in special need of attention. Family groups may arrange their affairs to spend their vacation time each year in territory where the need is greater, using a portion of each day for the field ministry. Many who have done this report that these are the most refreshing and delightful vacations that they have had anywhere. Some individuals and families have even moved into these areas to live, so that they can advance the Kingdom interests where the need is particularly great. They are like the apostle Paul, who, having worked hard to preach and build up congregations in one area, was anxious to move out into new fields.—Rom. 15:23, 24.

Are you in position to take up service where the need is greater in the country where you are now living? Then feel free to write to the Society's office for suggestions on locations. Tell the Society the name of your congregation, your age, date of baptism, what servant's position you have in the congregation and whether you are married and have a family. If you have in mind a particular section of the country, be sure to mention this in your letter. If your desire is to move to another country to serve, write directly to the branch office responsible for the territory in which you are interested. Such a move requires careful planning and strong reliance on Jehovah; it can also bring rich blessings.

REGULAR PIONEER SERVICE

Another privilege that is open to qualified ministers is the regular pioneer service, in which one devotes a hundred or more hours each month to the field ministry. Is this something that you could do? It is not really difficult. Just three hours and twenty minutes a day, on an average, needs to be set aside for the actual field service, and the rest of the day remains in which you can care for other responsibilities. You may serve either in your home territory or elsewhere. With careful planning, many thousands of Jehovah's witnesses find that they can do it, and they rejoice to be able to express their love for Jehovah so fully.

This is a field of service to which every young person ought to give serious consideration. When he completes his years of required secular education, what is he going to do with his life? Does he truly love Jehovah and has he made an unreserved dedication of himself to God? Then there should be no doubt. He will serve Jehovah to the full.

It is true, there are some young folks who find themselves confronted with heavy responsibilities because of unfortunate situations that have developed at home; others have severe physical limitations. (1 Tim. 5:4) They may build their lives around their ministry, but their circumstances limit to some extent what they are able to do in the direct field ministry. Yet no one, young or old, who truly loves God will shove the ministry into a secondary place so that he can devote the best of his time and effort to other activity simply because he prefers it. (Matt. 6:24, 33; 1 John 2: 15) When he got baptized in symbol of his dedication he was, in effect, saying before all observers that he loved Jehovah with all his heart and mind and soul and strength and that, more than anything else, he wanted to devote himself to the service of God. Now, is he backing up that profession by works?—Luke 10:25-28; Ps. 40:8.

Pioneer service is not limited to any certain age-group. The pioneer ranks include young and old, single and married, the physically strong and some who have limited resources of health. Most of them had obstacles to overcome in order to become pioneers. But deep-seated love for Jehovah, full reliance on him and careful planning have made it possible for tens of thousands to enjoy the pioneer ministry. The field ministry is not all that there is to our lives as Christians, and other Scriptural obligations cannot be ignored simply because one prefers the field service. But those who, on examining their own situation, find that they can make adjustments in their lives to become pioneers, and who do so out of love, will enjoy rich blessings at the hand of God.

Do you qualify to be a pioneer? There are certain pre-enrollment requirements to be met. One should have been a baptized minister for at least six months, and he should be a regular publisher, having reported service each month for the past six months. His field service averages for the past half year should show at least ten hours and six back-calls and he should currently be conducting a home Bible study. Also, he should have a reputation for fine Christian conduct.

If you meet these requirements, you may obtain an application blank from your overseer, the circuit servant or the Society. Read it carefully and answer all the questions. Then, at least thirty days before you desire to start pioneering, submit the application to your congregation overseer for consideration by the committee. He will check it for accuracy, and the committee will fill in its recommendation. If you meet the qualifications set out in the preceding paragraph, they will recommend that the Society accept your application. However, if anyone is presently on probation for unchristian conduct, uses tobacco or does not have a reputation as a fine example of a Christian, they kindly inform the applicant that they cannot recommend him and they do not send the application to the Society. In some situations, there may be doubt in the minds of the committee members; so they submit the application to the Society along with a statement of the factors that bear on the case, and, of course, the Society makes the decision. If anyone's application is not approved by the Society, the Society will notify that person directly. But if you are appointed by the Society to be a regular pioneer, notification of appointment will be sent to your overseer so that he can make announcement to the congregation, and he will give you all the supplies sent for your use.

Your application to be a pioneer is also an expression of willingness to accept the responsibilities that go with that special service. Pioneers are expected to devote at least 100 hours to the field ministry each month, on the average, or 1,200 hours a year. And, because they are spending much time in the service, they are urged to make it their goal to place at least 100 magazines each month, make 35 back-calls and conduct 7 home Bible studies each week. Promptly at the end of the month, a pioneer report card is to be filled out and handed to the congregation servant. He has the figures from it noted on your Publisher's Record card in the congregation file, signs your report card and mails it to the Society no later than the third of the month. If, for some reason, you are unable to report a full 100 hours for certain months, a note of explanation should be included on your report card and then you should arrange to make up the time before the service year ends, so that your total report for the entire service year, which runs from September 1 through the following August 31, will be at least 1,200 hours. As for your Bible study reports, these are to be turned in to the congregation each month for the Bible study file, though the congregation will not count them in its report, since you have already reported them to the Society.

Those pioneers living in isolated territory send their reports directly to the Society, including on them a notation of any public meetings held in the territory and any persons baptized during the month. In their case, so that there will be a record of their service available for consultation during the visit of the circuit servant, they need to keep their weekly record sheets for at least a year.

Participation in the field ministry and submitting regular reports are not all that is involved in being a pioneer. As is true of all of Jehovah's witnesses, pioneers need to work closely with Jehovah's organization, cooperate with the appointed servants and benefit fully from the meetings provided. Furthermore, as an appointee of the Society, each pioneer ought to be keenly aware of his responsibility to be exemplary in Christian conduct. He should refrain from any activity that might result in reproach to the name of God and to the congregation of His people. (2 Cor. 6:3, 4) Any pioneer who commits an act of sexual immorality with another person will be removed from the pioneer ranks for at least a year, even if he is not disfellowshiped, and the same is true if he engages in any other conduct that would necessitate his removal if he were an appointed servant in the congregation. Pioneers are to be exemplary ministers.

Each one who is a pioneer must determine for himself how much secular work he needs to do in order to care for his physical needs. The apostle Paul set a fine example by working with his hands so as not to impose an expensive burden on the congregation in whose territory he served. (Acts 18:2-4; 20:33, 34; 2 Thess. 3:7, 8) However, he made the ministry his chief concern, and did only what tentmaking was required to provide the physical necessities of life. Pioneers do well to follow that example, "seeking first the kingdom" and looking to God to bless their efforts to obtain the food and covering that they require. (Matt. 6:33) To aid pioneers to meet their expenses, the Society provides them with literature at less than cost.

When a pioneer desires a change of assignment because of moving or because he will be in another location for more than three months, he returns his pioneer assignment card to the Society and requests reassignment. The same procedure is followed when a congregation divides and the pioneer finds himself in the territory of the newly formed group. But if he is going to be away visiting for only three months or less, no change is required, and he will continue to send his report card to his congregation at the end of each month to be forwarded to the Society. Pioneers who move to another country, with the intention of staying for more than three months, request the Society to transfer their records to the branch office under which they will be serving, and then they arrange with that branch office for assignment in the area where they would like to work.

Anyone who finds it necessary to leave the pioneer ranks may do so by returning his pioneer identification and assignment card to the Society. Sometimes circumstances arise in one's life that make this necessary. But, wherever possible, we encourage those in the pioneer ministry to make it their career, staying with it, just as Jesus continued full time in the preaching work down to the time of his death.

VACATION PIONEER SERVICE

There are many of Jehovah's witnesses who, after honestly appraising their personal circumstances, do not find that they can be regular pioneers. But they are able to be vacation pioneers from time to time. It takes careful planning on their part and extra effort, but their love for Jehovah moves them to do it when they can. Many share in this activity during the month of April each year, when there is much special activity in the congregations. Others do it during those months when the circuit servant visits their congregation, or at vacation time or at regular intervals all year long. For them, these are the happiest and most spiritually stimulating months of the year.

Have you considered enrolling as a vacation pioneer? The requirements are not difficult. To qualify for appointment, you must be baptized and be a regular publisher (which means that you have reported field service during each of the past six months), and you must be given a favorable recommendation by the congregation committee. Applications are handled in the same manner as was described in connection with regular pioneer service.

It is possible to enroll as a vacation pioneer for two consecutive weeks, or for one, two or more months. Those who apply agree to devote at least 100 hours to the field service each full month that they are vacation pioneers, and two-week vacation pioneers agree to spend not less than 75 hours in the field ministry for the month. These service goals can easily be met by arranging for four hours of service each day of the month or three or four eight-hour days of service each week.

At the end of the month those who are vacation pioneers each fill out a report card and hand it to their overseer. He has the information listed on each one's Publisher's Record card, with a notation that the individual was a vacation pioneer. The report cards are then signed and sent to the Society by the third of the month.

If you have not yet been a vacation pioneer, we urge you to do so. This is a special service that is within the reach of nearly every Christian minister at some time during the year. Most publishers who do it once are anxious to do it again.

SPECIAL PIONEER SERVICE

Pioneers whose record of service shows that they are getting results in their ministry and who are free to move to any assignment where they are needed may be invited by the Society to become special pioneers. Some are assigned to work with congregations that have much territory that is not being regularly covered, but usually they go into isolated territory to carry on the preaching work and organize new congregations.

For best results, they select a well-populated portion of their territory and work it thoroughly, covering it again and again. They follow through on all who show interest and patiently conduct studies with them, at the same time keeping the house-to-house work going on a regular basis. Gradually they try to get those attending the home Bible studies acquainted with one another. In time one of the newly interested persons may be willing to open his home for a study that others are welcome to attend. This provides the basis for a meeting much like the congregation book studies that are sponsored by every congregation. To stimulate the gathering of newly interested ones, public meetings are planned periodically. Then, as the group manifests readiness to progress, arrangements are made for the *Watchtower* study and other congregation meetings, one at a time. Special care is given to acquaint these people with Jehovah's organization and how it operates. The privilege of participating in the field service is always kept before them, and, when they qualify, they are trained in the preaching work. This requires patient, steady work. When men who are associated with the group get baptized, special attention is given to training them so that they will be able to assume responsibility as servants in a congregation. Then, when the congregation is organized, the special pioneer stays with it to build it up until it is firmly established and able to continue making good progress with Jehovah's blessing.—Acts 20: 17-21, 31; 19:1, 8-10.

From this it can readily be seen that qualifications for special pioneer service include ability to conduct productive home Bible studies, a good knowledge of Jehovah's organization and willingness to stay with an assignment until it is done. Those are qualifications that all of us should have, and they will help to make your ministry more fruitful no matter where you serve.

Those who accept assignments of service as special pioneers agree to devote 150 hours to the field ministry each month, and they endeavor to place 150 magazines a month. They also put much emphasis on follow-up work, striving to make 50 back-calls each month and to conduct 10 home Bible studies weekly.

This full program of service leaves little time for secular work; so the Society supplies special pioneers with a nominal money allowance each month that 150 hours of field service and 50 back-calls are reported, to aid them in obtaining the needed "sustenance and covering." (1 Tim. 6:8) And, as is true of all other pioneers, they receive their literature supplies at less than cost. Additional financial assistance is given to special pioneers about November 1 each year to obtain clothing. These zealous ministers work hard, and at times a change is needed; so provision is made for them to take two weeks off each year, and if they have a record of continuous service in various branches of the pioneer work for twenty years, the vacation time is extended to three weeks.

The Society is keenly interested in the work of these brothers and keeps in touch with them, both by correspondence and through regular visits of the circuit servant. Each time around the circuit he spends a full week with them, helping them to analyze and organize their work, sharing together in every feature of service, doing personal study with them and having each of the congregation meetings during the course of the week. In this way they are strengthened and encouraged in their ministry. There are special joys in this work of opening up new territory and organizing congregations. It was in this type of service that the apostle Paul took pleasure, and the record of his ministry continues to be a source of inspiration to those who reach out for this privilege of service.—Rom. 15:20-24.

MISSIONARY SERVICE

Among the Christians of the first century there was a keen awareness of the need for missionaries who were willing to carry the message of salvation to foreign lands. After his resurrection, had not Jesus told an assembly of his disciples: "Go therefore and make disciples of people of all the nations"? (Matt. 28:19) And, immediately before his ascension to heaven, did he not say: "You will be witnesses of me both in Jerusalem and in all

Judea and Samaria and to the most distant part of the earth"? (Acts 1:8) In response, the apostle Peter traveled east as far as Babylon; the apostle John served in the Roman province of Asia; and Paul and his close associates penetrated into Europe in their missionary travels.

The need for missionaries is still great in our day, and it is gratifying to know that young men and women are taking up this work. Those who enter missionary service and stay there are not persons who indifferently reason that, after all, God could use someone else to do the job. To the contrary, their heartfelt love for Jehovah moves them to volunteer in the spirit of that faithful prophet Isaiah, who said: "Here I am! Send me." (Isa. 6:8) They know that the Kingdom good news is to be preached "in all the inhabited earth," and they are delighted to be used by God, having a full share in it. (Matt. 24:14) Their faith gives them the conviction that, no matter where they are on earth, Jehovah will look after them as long as they are busy doing his will.

Some have been missionaries for ten, fifteen or twenty years, and they love their work. But there is still much work to do, and they rejoice when they can welcome new missionaries into the field. Can you join them?

Those who are sent into missionary service by the Society are first given special training at the Watchtower Bible School of Gilead in Brooklyn, New York. Here they make an intensive study of the Bible, receive instruction in organizational matters and are helped to acquire a foundation knowledge of the language of the land to which they will be going.

The prospective missionaries who are invited to attend Gilead School are selected from among persons who meet the following qualifications: baptized at least three years; pioneering for the past two years; generally, between the ages of 21

and 40; single, or married at least two years and
with no dependent children. They must know the
English language. Those who apply should have
good health; they should be willing to serve anywhere; and they should plan to stay in their
missionary assignment, making it their home.
Applications may be requested directly from the
Society or they may be obtained and filled out at
special meetings arranged for this purpose at
most district assemblies.

Missionaries carry on their work in the same
way as do the special pioneers, and they have the
same service requirements to meet. However,
where possible, the Society provides a missionary
home from which a group of them can carry on
their work and sees to it that they are able to
obtain the needed food. In addition, each missionary is given some financial assistance once a year
to obtain clothing, as well as a small monthly
allowance for personal items, if he is meeting the
service requirements. There is also a vacation
provision each year, as for special pioneers. Because they are devoting all their time and effort
to advancing the interests of God's kingdom, Jehovah, through his organization, makes loving
provision to care for their physical needs.—Luke
12:22-31.

At first the customs and foods in another
country may seem strange, but soon one grows
accustomed to them. A loving desire to aid the
people to learn the truth about God and his kingdom makes any inconveniences of a changed way
of life pale out of sight. As one sees the truth of
God's Word bring about changes in their lives,
he cannot but be humbly thankful that Jehovah
has privileged him to have a share in the work.
What a thrill it has been to the missionaries to
see congregations grow up in the territory where
they serve, and to know that persons with whom
they studied have become publishers, pioneers,

congregation overseers and circuit servants! Jehovah has indeed blessed them because they have worked hard in his service and have done so with a willing heart.

Are you able to share in this urgent work? Do you qualify? Does your heart move you to do so? We urge you to give it serious consideration.

BETHEL SERVICE

In order to supply Jehovah's witnesses around the globe with Bibles and Bible literature for their personal study, for use in congregation meetings and for distribution in the field ministry, it is necessary for the Society to operate Bethel homes, branch offices and printing plants. Those who do the work at these places are all ordained ministers. Some have been in Bethel service for many years.

There is work of many kinds to be done by those at Bethel. Some have office assignments; others do typesetting, run printing presses, bind books or prepare literature for mailing. In addition, it is necessary to have workers who care for the home, wash clothes and cook and serve meals. All of this is done to further the Kingdom interests.

Much of this work is like that done by early Christians who are mentioned in the Bible. For example, Tertius and Silvanus did scribal work, recording portions of the Bible at the direction of the apostles Paul and Peter. (Rom. 16:22; 1 Pet. 5:12) Today brothers in Bethel service are privileged to print and bind copies of the Bible in many languages, and some run printing presses on which Scriptural counsel provided through the "faithful and discreet slave" is reproduced for the benefit of God's people everywhere. (Matt. 24: 45-47) Others serving in Bethel homes have assignments like that of Stephen and his associates, who, as waiters, 'distributed food to the tables' of early Christians who were serving together in Jerusalem. At the same time, the Bible informs us, Stephen had an outstanding record as a fearless preacher of the Word of God.—Acts 6:1-10.

Bethel family members start their day's activity early. Gathered at the breakfast table, they enjoy a thorough discussion of the day's Scripture text and comments. After breakfast they go to their assigned work, at which they spend at least 8 hours and 40 minutes a day for five days of the week, and four hours on Saturdays. Monday evenings the members of the family study the *Watchtower* lesson for the week and attend the family's Theocratic Ministry School. Other evenings as well as Saturday afternoon and Sunday are used for attending congregation meetings, sharing in the field ministry and attending to personal matters. Many brothers at Bethel serve as congregation overseers or ministerial servants, and those who are qualified speakers have the privilege of giving public talks in nearby congregations. The schedule is a full one and richly rewarding in a spiritual way.

Applicants for Bethel service must be dedicated and baptized ministers for at least a year, and preference is shown for those who are pioneers. The work to be done requires good health, ability to do hard work and willingness to do whatever is assigned. Most of the ones invited to live and work at Bethel are single brothers, between seventeen and thirty-five years of age; though at times sisters are invited, and some married couples without dependent children. Anyone who applies for Bethel service should have deep love for Jehovah, his Word and his organization, and a strong desire to serve on behalf of his Christian brothers. The ones whose applications are accepted agree to serve at Bethel for a minimum of four years, but any who can do so are encouraged to stay beyond that and make service at Bethel their life's work. If you meet these qualifications and want to serve at Bethel, you may obtain an application from a circuit servant, from the Society or at one of the meetings arranged for Bethel applicants at most district assemblies.

The Society takes good care of the members of the Bethel family. They are provided with a comfortable room and good food. There is a small monthly allowance to care for personal expenses, and each year financial assistance is provided to help them to obtain needed clothing. Time is also allowed for a two-week vacation, and three weeks for those who have served for twenty years or more. The physical provisions to sustain them are made possible through the contributions of Jehovah's witnesses world wide to the Watch Tower Bible and Tract Society, and the Bethel family appreciates these things.

Bethel is a marvelous place to serve. In such a theocratic atmosphere as exists at Bethel homes there is excellent opportunity for spiritual growth. It is richly rewarding to work all day in association with others who love Jehovah and to know that one's work benefits so many of Jehovah's people.

Of course, not everyone in Jehovah's organization is in position to share in Bethel service; nor are all able to be pioneers. But each one can walk in the footsteps of Jesus Christ, whose whole purpose in life was the doing of his Father's will. Love of God moves one to keep Jehovah's service in first place and to plan everything else in life around it. If our share in the preaching work is somewhat limited, let us be sure that it is because of circumstances over which we have no control and not because of indifference. If we have been entrusted with special assignments of service, let us be watchful so that they do not become commonplace but that we cherish them as privileges extended to us by God. No matter where we serve, we cannot afford to let ourselves become complacent, reasoning that we are having at least some share in Jehovah's service and, after all, that is the important thing. Whole-souled service is what pleases God. So it is wise for each one of us to examine his service to God and to search his heart. Do as the Bible counsels: "Keep testing whether you are in the faith, keep proving what you yourselves are."—2 Cor. 13:5.

CHAPTER 12

Endurance Needed to Gain Everlasting Life

Acts 5:27

BECAUSE you permit God's Word to light your path, you have dedicated yourself to Jehovah God and symbolized that by water immersion. With that Word as your guide, you have become an ordained minister of God, and now you have before you the prospect of eternal life in the satisfying service of God. But the foremost enemy of God and man does not want you to gain that prize. As the apostle Peter wrote to fellow members of the Christian congregation: "Your adversary, the Devil, walks about like a roaring lion, seeking to devour someone." (1 Pet. 5:8) He would like to destroy your spirituality, cause you to cease serving Jehovah and so bring you to ruin. It is most appropriate, therefore, that the Bible cautions us: "You have need of endurance, in order that, after you have done the will of God, you may receive the fulfillment of the promise."—Heb. 10:36.

To endure, you must never lose sight of the fact that the warfare in which you are engaged is a spiritual one. Your principal foes are "wicked spirit forces in the heavenly places." Therefore, if you are going to come off victorious, you must make full use of the provisions that Jehovah has made. You need to "go on acquiring power in the Lord and in the mightiness of his strength." (Eph. 6:10-13) How can this be done?

Jehovah has provided his written Word, and daily study and meditation on it will help to fortify both your mind and your heart. It will keep God's thoughts to the fore in your life, so that decisions will be in harmony with his will. If you heed what you learn from the Bible, you will also stay close to Jehovah's organization, regularly attending and sharing in the meetings. This will prevent you from getting into a position where, by yourself, you are easy prey for the enemy. Regular participation in the field ministry is also important. If one is going to endure, he surely cannot afford to allow himself to become indifferent about the work that God has given his people to do.

But some have done that. They may have reported some field service from time to time in the past; yet they were not persons who made a habit of attending all the congregation meetings. They were weak spiritually. When assistance was offered, they did not respond fully. In their case it was just a short step to inactivity. Failing to "go on acquiring power in the Lord," they fell easy victims to the pressures of the Adversary.

There are others who at one time shared to a considerable extent in the ministry, but then they too slowed down, reasoning that perhaps it is not so vital to preach since God is going to resurrect the vast majority of people anyway. In doing so, are they really walking in the footsteps of Jesus Christ? Do they view the matter as he did? When Jesus was here on earth, he was well aware of the fact that the majority of those to whom he preached would be raised up on Judgment Day. (Matt. 11:20-24) Did he conclude that this made his preaching work really unimportant? By no means! He devoted all his time to it, and so did his apostles. Why? As Jesus reported to his Father in prayer on the last night of his life as a human: "I have glorified you on the earth, having finished the work you have given me to do." (John 17:4) That is why Jesus preached —to glorify his Father. Is that why you share in the preaching work? If so, the fact that God will raise the dead does not lessen the importance of preaching; it gives added reason to publicly praise the name of God. "Give thanks to Jehovah, you people, for he is good; for his loving-kindness is to time indefinite." (Ps. 118:1) Strong love for Jehovah and an earnest desire to see his name magnified will stimulate you to press on in his service.

Nor should we minimize the importance of the preaching work in relation to the salvation of those to whom we preach now. This generation faces the downfall of Babylon the Great and the war of Armageddon. Jehovah has set a time limit, and the opportunity to choose his side of the issue of universal sovereignty is now! There is no promise in God's Word of a resurrection for those destroyed by his Executioner at the conclusion of this wicked system of things, now near at hand. Their failure to take note of impending destruction will not save them. The destruction will be everlasting. (Matt. 24:38, 39; 2 Thess. 1:6-10) If they are going to be delivered, they must hear the warning message now, believe it and call in faith upon the name of Jehovah.—Joel 2:32; Rom. 10:13-15.

Of course, not all are going to respond favorably. Many will be indifferent; some will be unkind. Their attitude will require endurance on your part so that you do not get discouraged and quit. Regularly reviewing the fine examples of faithful endurance recorded in the Bible can help you. Is your territory as difficult as Noah's was? In all the years that he preached before the Flood, only his own wife, his sons and their wives joined with him in doing the will of God. The world scoffed, but Noah did "according to all that God had commanded him." Jehovah preserved Noah and his household when that "world of ungodly people" was destroyed, and he will preserve you at the end of this system of things if you endure as Noah did.—Gen. 6:22; 2 Pet. 2:5, 9.

The prophet Jeremiah was another one who had a difficult assignment. For forty years he preached to people who professed to serve the true God but who ignored His commandments. They did not approve of Jeremiah's work, but Jehovah did. (Jer. 1:7, 8) With faith in Jehovah, Jeremiah endured. Faith in God will also enable you to endure. So do not let the unresponsive attitude of other people cause you to slack off in your service to God. Some will appreciate the message that you bring to them; others will reject it. But Jehovah's blessing will be on you if, now that you have heard the word of God, you "retain it and bear fruit with endurance."—Luke 8:15.

An even more severe test of your devotion to God and Christ may be brought to bear by those who are members of your own family. Jesus warned: "I came to cause division, with a man against his father, and a daughter against her mother, and a young wife against her mother-in-law. Indeed, a man's enemies will be persons of his own household." He knew that family members would in many cases react with opposition against the one who embraced his teachings. Has that occurred among your relatives? If so, it puts you to the test. Which is the stronger tie, the controlling one in your life? Is it your attitude toward your family that dictates your attitude toward God? Or is it your love of God and Christ that influences how you deal with your family?

(Matt. 10:32-37) There is only one right way. Forsaking God is not going to bring benefits to anyone. Not only does it result in loss to the quitter, but it removes from the home the fine influence that might have aided others there to gain salvation. (1 Cor. 7:16) Manifesting the fruits of God's spirit in your coping with difficult situations will help you to endure, and, as Jesus said to his disciples, "by endurance on your part you will acquire your souls."—Luke 21:19.

Even though your fleshly relatives do not encourage you in the service of God, there are many who do. As one of Jehovah's witnesses you enjoy association with a large family under the loving headship of Jehovah God. The psalmist David wrote: "In case my own father and my own mother did leave me, even Jehovah himself would take me up." (Ps. 27:10) And Jesus himself said: "No one has left house or brothers or sisters or mother or father or children or fields for my sake and for the sake of the good news who will not get a hundredfold now in this period of time, houses and brothers and sisters and mothers and children and fields, with persecutions, and in the coming system of things everlasting life." (Mark 10:29, 30) Regular fellowship with these spiritual brothers and sisters of yours will build you up. It will keep you strong in faith and help you to endure, with everlasting life in view.

Living as we do in a world where the spirit of nationalism is strong, we ought to expect that from this quarter too our faith will be put to the test. In fact, the book of Revelation, after discussing in symbolic language God's view of this situation, says: "Here is where it means endurance for the holy ones, those who observe the commandments of God and the faith of Jesus." (Rev. 14: 9-12) The "holy ones" have repeatedly had their faith put to the test on this issue, and their "other sheep" companions are now being called on to manifest their faithful endurance in connection with the same issue. Do they really take to heart Jesus' statement concerning his disciples: "You are no part of the world"? (John 15:19) Do they really believe that all the kingdoms of the world lie in the power of the wicked one, Satan the Devil? (Luke 4:5-8; 1 John 5:19; Rev. 13:1, 2) Is their full confidence in the kingdom of God, now established in the heavens in the hands of Jesus Christ? If they have that faith, it will fortify them to endure without compromise when put to the test; because "this is the conquest that has conquered the world, our faith."—1 John 5:4.

Tests may come because of wars, revolutions or outright persecution and official bans, which may make it impossible for you to carry on Christian worship in all the details outlined in this book. It may be impossible to hold large congregation meetings. Contact with the Society may temporarily be broken off. Visits by circuit servants may be interrupted for a while. New publications may not arrive. If any of these things happen to you, what should you do? The answer is: Do whatever you can in the way of pure worship under the circumstances. Personal study should be possible. Usually small groups of brothers can meet for study in homes. Publications that were studied in the past, along with the Bible, can be used as a basis for meetings. Experience has shown that some form of worship is possible even in times of difficulty; so do not become excited or worried. Generally in a short time some form of communication with Jehovah's visible organization will be established, because the Society always seeks to find ways of getting in touch with the brothers. But even if you find yourself isolated from all your Christian brothers, keep in mind that you are not isolated from Jehovah. He can still hear your prayers and he can strengthen you with his spirit. Look to him for guidance. Remember that you are a minister, and, as opportunities to witness to others open up, make good use of them. Jehovah will bless your efforts, and others may soon join you in worship.—Phil. 1:27-30; 4:6, 7; 2 Tim. 4:16-18; Acts 4:13-31; 5:27-42.

That it is not one's own strength but one's trust in Jehovah that enables one to hold firm in the face of pressures brought by Satan is particularly driven home when one's life is threatened by opposers of pure worship. Of his own experience in this regard, the apostle Paul wrote to the congregation of God in Corinth: "We do not wish you to be ignorant, brothers, about the tribulation that happened to us in the district of Asia, that we were under extreme pressure beyond our strength, so that we were very uncertain even of our lives. In fact, we felt within ourselves that we had received the sentence of death. This was that we might have our trust, not in ourselves, but in the God who raises up the dead. From such a great thing as death he did rescue us and will rescue us; and our hope is in him that he will also rescue us further."—2 Cor. 1:8-10.

Do you have such strong trust in "the God who raises up the dead"? There is every reason for you to do so, because God has raised Christ from the dead and through him made provision for resurrection of others of mankind. The threat of death has been one of the foremost methods used by Satan to hold men in bondage, but Christ died "that he might emancipate all those who for fear of death were subject to slavery all through their lives." (Heb. 2:15) Your faith in this provision of the resurrection can help you to endure even the most severe opposition.—Luke 21:19.

Whether the trials of your faith are great or apparently small, remember that Jehovah is always near to sustain you. Look to him for guidance and for the strength to stand firm. Instead of asking yourself, 'Can I endure?' pray to Jehovah,

'Strengthen me to endure, for your own name's sake.' Jesus prayed earnestly to his Father when under trial, and he urged his disciples to do the same.—Heb. 5:7; Luke 22:40.

Consider carefully the fine example set by Jesus Christ. At Hebrews 12:2, 3 it is recorded: "For the joy that was set before him he endured a torture stake, despising shame, and has sat down at the right hand of the throne of God. Indeed, consider closely the one who has endured such contrary talk by sinners against their own interests, that you may not get tired and give out in your souls." What Jesus did is not something that you cannot do. As the Scriptures show, he provided a model for you, when under suffering, to follow his steps closely. (1 Pet. 2:21) When faced with severe tests he kept in focus the outcome of the situation. He knew that faithfulness on his part would result in honor to Jehovah, and in this he found joy. He realized, too, that his faithfulness under test would strengthen others to endure, and he had their interests at heart. (John 16:33) Also, he rejoiced in the prospects of future service in Jehovah's organization that would be his as a reward for his integrity-keeping course. (John 17: 4, 5) Doing these things will also strengthen you.

The Bible makes clear to us that the trials of one's faith are not limited to opposition from other persons. The Devil has other methods, too, and we need to be on guard against them if we are to gain everlasting life. Surely we do not want to manifest traits that are in any way comparable to those displayed by the Devil. But on every hand such traits are displayed by the world around us, and if we are not on guard we may adopt them. How that would please the Devil! He himself is proud, self-willed and rebellious, and when humans develop those characteristics he is able to use them as his tools. (1 Tim. 3:6; Eph. 2:2) This is why God's Word admonishes: "Quit being fashioned after this system of things, but be transformed by making your mind over, that you may prove to yourselves the good and acceptable and perfect will of God."—Rom. 12:2.

If we do this, we will carefully avoid any tendencies toward pride. (Jas. 4:16) We will not become faultfinders or complainers, either about the provisions that Jehovah makes for his people or about our own lot in life. (Num. 11:1; 1 Cor. 10:10; Jude 16) Never will we give in to a spirit of self-will or rebellion. (2 Pet. 2:10; 1 Sam. 15:23) Rather, by seeking the help of Jehovah's spirit and putting forth a sincere effort to respond to it, we will cultivate qualities that are well-pleasing in the eyes of God. (Eph. 5:8-18) We will learn to put full trust in Jehovah and show ourselves ready to obey the counsel of his Word. (Prov. 3:5; Jas. 3:17) We will be humble, not thinking more of ourselves than we ought to think and not overestimating the value of our own opinions. (Prov. 22:4; Rom. 12:3) We will be cooperative with all our brothers and submissive to the leading of the "faithful and discreet slave" and those overseers with whom we are more closely associated. (Matt. 24:45-47; Heb. 13:17; 1 Cor. 16:16; 2 Cor. 9:13) This will be a protection to us. It will keep us close to Jehovah and to his organization. It will make our service a joy, and so will aid us to endure.

Another snare of the Devil is materialism. Some who stand firm in the face of persecution later give in to the lure of materialistic desires. The Bible warns: "The love of money is a root of all sorts of injurious things, and by reaching out for this love some have been led astray from the faith and have stabbed themselves all over with many pains." But that does not have to happen to you, and it will not if you recognize the danger and act in harmony with the admonition that is given next in the Bible: "You, O man of God, flee from these things." Do not toy with them. Do not fool yourself, allowing materialistic desires to dominate your life while you make a pretense of serving God. "Where your treasure is, there your heart will be also. . . . You cannot slave for God and for Riches." Instead of allowing a love for material possessions to take hold of your heart, "pursue righteousness, godly devotion, faith, love, endurance, mildness of temper. Fight the fine fight of the faith, get a firm hold on the everlasting life for which you were called and you offered the fine public declaration in front of many witnesses."—1 Tim. 6:10-12; Matt. 6:21, 24.

As you face and pass each test of endurance, it will strengthen you to meet others. But do not grow overconfident. Remember that, although the Israelites were delivered from Egypt, "on most of them God did not express his approval, for they were laid low in the wilderness." Not all died for the same reason. But even after long years in the wilderness, just before they were to cross the Jordan River into the Promised Land, a large number fell into a trap of Satan and lost out. They got involved in sexual immorality. Concerning this, Paul wrote: "Neither let us practice fornication, as some of them committed fornication, only to fall, twenty-three thousand of them in one day. . . . Now these things went on befalling them as examples, and they were written for a warning to us upon whom the ends of the systems of things have arrived. Consequently let him that thinks he is standing beware that he does not fall." (1 Cor. 10:5, 8-12) If we would endure, we cannot afford to become careless. We must keep on seeking, not only God's kingdom, but also his righteousness. —Matt. 6:33.

Regular attendance at the meetings of the congregation with which you are associated will aid you immeasurably to keep strong your love of righteousness. It will help you to stay close to

Jehovah and active in his service. With a view to faithful endurance, take seriously the Bible's admonition not to forsake gathering with the Christian congregation for worship. To the extent possible, prepare for those meetings and participate in them. Include all of them in your program of activity. If you plan to move to another community, find out in advance where the nearest congregation is and when the meetings are held. With everlasting life in view, stay close to those who are walking in the way that will lead to that reward. Regardless of how often you have attended congregation meetings, the Scriptures encourage you to do it "all the more so as you behold the day drawing near."—Heb. 10:24, 25.

It is not only this year that we must be faithful to Jehovah, but next year and the year after that, yes, "from now on and to time indefinite." (Ps. 115:18) We dedicated ourselves to serve him, not for just a few years, but forever. In response to Jehovah's direction, Abraham left behind the comforts of Ur of Chaldea for life in tents in another land. He did not grow weary in five or ten years and return to the life that he had left behind. He showed endurance, living as a temporary resident for a hundred years, while awaiting in faith "the city having real foundations, the builder and creator of which city is God." (Heb. 11:10) Have you endured that long? No, but the endurance that you have shown because of your love of God is pleasing to him, and, if you continue faithful, it will be your happy privilege to prove faithful to God, not just a hundred years or even a thousand, but forever.

You have need of endurance. But you were not born with it, and it is not something that you can acquire as a gift. It comes as a result of having your faith put to the test. For that reason, the disciple James wrote: "Consider it all joy, my brothers, when you meet with various trials, knowing as you do that this tested quality of your faith works out endurance. But let endurance have its work complete, that you may be complete and sound in all respects, not lacking in anything." (Jas. 1:2-4) So those experiences through which Satan means to tear you down can, in fact, build you up. Instead of causing you to lose out, they can produce in you a quality that wins Jehovah's approval. Understandably, then, Paul wrote: "Let us exult while in tribulations, since we know that tribulation produces endurance; endurance, in turn, an approved condition." (Rom. 5:3, 4) What a happy reversal of matters that is!

It becomes plain, then, that in order to endure we must always look to God's inspired Word for guidance. We need to work closely with the organization that he is using to accomplish his will. We need to make full use of the privilege of prayer. If we do so, we will persevere in the work that the resurrected Jesus Christ set out for all his disciples when he said: "Go therefore and make disciples of people of all the nations, baptizing them in the name of the Father and of the Son and of the holy spirit, teaching them to observe all the things I have commanded you." (Matt. 28:19, 20) Having applied ourselves wholeheartedly to that work during this period of time, we will be blessed with the opportunity to serve Jehovah everlastingly in his righteous new order. That happy prospect is yours if you persevere in proving by your way of life now that you concur with the psalmist in saying to Jehovah our God: "Your word is a lamp to my foot, and a light to my roadway."—Ps. 119: 105.

RECORD OF CHRISTIAN BAPTISM

As one of Jehovah's Christian witnesses I appreciate that the holy Bible is the written Word of God and that it must be "a lamp to my foot, and a light to my roadway." (Ps. 119:105) I am firmly convinced that "Jehovah is righteous in all his ways," and it is my earnest desire to live in full harmony with his will as he has made it plain to his servants. (Ps. 145:17) For that reason I have dedicated myself without reservation to Jehovah God through Jesus Christ to be his possession and do his will both now and for all time to come.

I have carefully studied "Basic Teachings of the Bible" as set out in this book, [Name] ....
....
personally reviewed them with me to be sure that I understand them, and I am in full agreement with them. Now I want to go on growing in knowledge, because I believe what Jesus Christ said as recorded in John 17:3 : "This means everlasting life, their taking in knowledge of you, the only true God, and of the one whom you sent forth, Jesus Christ." It is also my desire to work closely with Jehovah's visible organization.

In accord with the example and commandment of our Lord Jesus Christ, on [Date] ....
at [Place] ....
I was baptized in water. (Matt. 3:13-17; 28:19) I am now an ordained minister of Jehovah God and, with his blessing, I will have as full a share as possible in helping others to come to know him as the true God, that they too may love and serve him.

....
(Personal signature)

....
(Congregation overseer)

....
(Name of congregation)   (Date)

INDEX

221